NEVER TOO LATE

JOHN HOLT

NEVER TOO LATE

My Musical Life Story

A MERLOYD LAWRENCE BOOK

▲
▼▼

ADDISON-WESLEY PUBLISHING COMPANY, INC.
Reading, Massachusetts   Menlo Park, California   New York
Don Mills, Ontario   Wokingham, England   Amsterdam
Bonn   Sydney   Singapore   Tokyo   Madrid   San Juan
Paris   Seoul   Milan   Mexico City   Taipei

A portion of this work first appeared in *Atlantic Monthly*.

Lyrics from "Yes Sir, That's My Baby" by Gus Kahn and Walter Donaldson: Copyright © 1925 by Bourne Co. Copyright renewed. Used by permission. Used by permission of Traubner & Flynn.

Lyrics from the football song of "Jack Armstrong, the All American Boy": Used by permission of General Mills, Inc.

Lyrics from "When the Bloom Is on the Sage" by Fred Howard and Nat Vincent: Copyright 1930 by Morse M. Preeman. Copyright renewed 1957 by Southern Music Publishing Co., Inc. Used by permission.

Many of the designations used by manufacturers and sellers to distinguish their products are claimed as trademarks. Where those designations appear in this book and Addison-Wesley was aware of a trademark claim, the designations have been printed in initial capital letters (e.g., Ping-Pong).

Library of Congress Cataloging-in-Publication Data

Holt, John Caldwell, 1923–1985
    Never too late : my musical autobiography / John Holt.
        p.   cm.
    Reprint. Originally published: New York : Delacorte, 1978.
    "A Merloyd Lawrence book."
    ISBN 0-201-56763-6
    1. Holt, John Caldwell, 1923–1985.   2. Musicians—United States—
Biography.   I. Title.
ML419.H64A3   1991
780'.92—dc20   91-13202
  [B]   CIP
                                                       MN

Cover design by Linda Koegel

1 2 3 4 5 6 7 8 9-MW-9594939291
First Addison-Wesley printing, July 1991

*To Arthur Landers, Harold Sproul,
Izler Solomon, musicians and Teachers*

My warm thanks to my editor, Merloyd Lawrence, whose understanding, support, and sensible and helpful comments have made this a better book.

Contents

Introduction:
How and Why

Most people who play a musical instrument learned as children. I did not. Few adults who have never played an instrument before take one up, least of all in middle age, and least of all a bowed string instrument (supposed to be the hardest). I am one who did. Though I came from a largely nonmusical family and had almost no musical training or experience while growing up, I began to play the flute at thirty-four, and the cello at forty, which I put aside a couple of years later and then took up again at fifty. Now, when home, I try to play three or four hours a day, more when I can make time for it. To become a skillful musician has become perhaps the most important task of my life.

This book is the story of how it all came about. Friends of mine to whom I have told some of this story have found it interesting; I write it in the hope that others may, as well. I hope, too, that my story may encourage or help other people, above all adults, who may have thought they were too old, to begin to sing or to play a musical instrument. Or, that it may help many adults who are now amateur musicians to play better and enjoy it more. Perhaps teachers of adults may also find these words useful. Beyond this, musicians talk a great deal about ways to interest more people in music; perhaps my own experience, as told here, may suggest some ways to do this.

In a broader sense, this is a book about exploration and discovery. I have long had two favorite proverbs: one is Shaw's "Be sure to get what you like, or else you will have to like what you get," the other a translation from an old Spanish proverb, " 'Take what you want,' says God, 'and pay for it.' " To find out what one really wants, and what it costs, and how to pay what it costs, is an important part of everyone's life work. But it is not easy to find out what we like or want, when all our lives other people have been hard at work trying not just to make us do what they want, but to make us think that we *want* to do it. How then *do* we find out what we want? What sort of clues, experiences, inner messages, may tell us? What do we do about such messages when we get them? This is in part a book about such messages.

This is also a book about teaching, above all the teaching of music. Some music teachers have been enormously helpful to me—one of them, in ways I was not to realize for many years. But for the most part I am self-taught in music, and this book is also about that self-teaching. Part of the art of learning any difficult act, like music, is knowing both how to teach yourself and how best to use the teaching of others, how to gain from the greater experience and skill of other people without becoming dependent on them. For few people are likely to become good at music, or anything else, who do not learn how to teach themselves. What we can best learn from good teachers is *how* to teach ourselves better. Other learners of music may find here some things to help them become better self-teachers, and teachers of music may find ways to help their students do this.

In my journey into music I have been much helped by good fortune. As a child I may have been musically underprivileged (though no more so than most children) but I was in all other ways privileged. My parents (like their parents) were well-off; we lived in suburbs, not musically very lively but in all other ways easy and comfortable. I went to a "good" boarding school and college. As an adult I have been even more fortunate. If by choice I have lived much of my life with very little money, so that I could do work I believed in, I have also lived without many worries about money. This was partly because, though not through choice, or at least not *my* choice, I never married. Also, like most people who grow up rich, I never really believed that economic disaster could strike me. I know the dangers of poverty, as I know the dangers of the atomic bomb, but they have never been real to me in the way they are to people who have been poor, or to the survivors of Hiroshima and Nagasaki. Which is not to say, either, that poor people cannot learn to love music, or even to become musicians, even great musicians. Many have done so, and some are now doing so. J.B. Priestley once wrote that the working-class people he grew up with in Yorkshire knew more about music, and made more music, than the much richer working class of today. But it is certainly easier to explore, enjoy, and make music, as it is to do anything else, if one is not constantly worrying about money, and can afford such things as concerts, records, instruments, practice space, and lessons. The lack of these is one of the reasons why, to name just one example, the Greater Boston Youth Symphony hardly ever has in it any children from Boston. What we need to do, of course, is to make musical resources more available to people with little money.

A few years ago I read in the British magazine *The Gramophone* a short article about the noted German conductor Eugen Jochum. The article said that he had grown up in a town in Germany with a population of about two thousand, and that in that town there had been a symphony orchestra of 75 players and a mixed chorus of 150, who played and sang much of the great music. It may well be that this town was not typical, and that not every little German town had music making on this level. Still, if we had only one tenth this much music making here in Boston (or any town or city), we would have an orchestra in every neighborhood, and many quartets and chamber groups in every block. What a city, what a country that would be to live in! I would like to do all I can to bring that city and that country closer.

Another reason I am writing this book is to question the widely held idea that what happens to us in the first few years of our lives determines everything that will happen later, what we can be, what we can do. Musical people are particularly prone to talk this way. The great Japanese string teacher Suzuki, whose work I have long admired, writes in his books that if children do not hear, almost from birth, good music (by which he means classical music), if they hear, in short, the kind of popular music that was all I heard as a child, they will grow up tone deaf. Not so. Countless other teachers say that if we don't learn to play musical instruments as children we will never be able to learn as adults. Again, not so. Of course it is nice, if we come freely to music, to come to it young, but if we don't come to it then, we can later. It is never too late. And while there may be good grounds for saying that some music is "better" than other music—I happen to think that Beethoven is better than Hummel, Tchaikowsky better than Glazounov, Stravinsky better than John Cage, and Duke Ellington better than Glenn Miller—these distinctions have nothing to do with learning to love music. "Bad" music is not the enemy of "good" music. The world of music is very large, and all one piece; there are a great many roads into it. As long as we have access to all of it, and the right to explore it freely, making our judgments as we go, each of us can find his or her own way.

Most of all, I want to combat the idea that any disciplined and demanding activity, above all music, can never grow out of love, joy, and free choice, but must be rooted in forced exposure, coercion, and threat. Most of what I have read about music education says this one way or another. The idea is not only mistaken, but dangerous; nothing is more certain to make most people ignore or even hate great music than trying to ram more and more of it down the throats of more and more children in compulsory classes and lessons. The idea is wrong in a larger sense; in the long run, love and joy are more enduring sources of discipline and commitment than any amount of bribe and threat, and it is only what C. Wright Mills called the "crackpot realism" of our times that keeps us from seeing, or even being willing to see, that this is so.

Any other reasons I have for writing this book may become clearer as you read it.

1

A Week of Music

Monday

Monday is orchestra night. At about a quarter past six I put my cello and bow in their case, put music stand, music, glasses, gadget to hold the cello peg, and other miscellaneous stuff into a small shoulder bag, sling it over one shoulder and the cello case over the other, and walk to the Charles Street subway station. At Harvard Square I climb the stairs to Massachusetts Avenue, walk through the Harvard Yard and then another half mile or so to the small public school in which we play. A few of the other players are already there, and have set up the chairs. I set up my music stand in front of the back two of the six chairs in the cello section, take out bow, cello, music, and other stuff, and start to tune up. If I don't get tuned up before the horn and trumpets get here, I never will, in this small gym, they make such a racket that I can't hear my own cello well enough to tune accurately.

One at a time, the good cellists come in, and set up to play in the four seats in front of me. We say a few words, but not many; we have only two hours in this little gym, and everyone else, like me, is in a hurry to tune up and warm up. Wind and brass players come in; soon the room is a confusion and uproar of many instruments tuning, practicing scales and arpeggios, or bits of the music. How in the world, I wonder, do the Boston Symphony cellists tune up with the trumpets and trombones tuning right behind them? (One of the BSO cellists, I am told, wears earplugs when he plays.) Our young and very talented conductor, Paul Hess, arrives, taps his baton for relative quiet, tells us what we will play first. We get out the music, the oboe plays an A, we all tune once more. The conductor holds up his baton (a skinny little white stick), and we begin.

It is a new piece, new for us, new certainly to me. I have a faint hope that since we are reading it through for the first time the conductor will take it at a slightly slower tempo, which will give me a chance to catch a few more of the notes. No such luck. We take it at full speed, faster, even, than many professional orchestras. Most of the players are considerably better than I am, and certainly better music readers; even if the music sounds a bit ragged, they are catching most of the notes. Ahead of me I can see the fingers and bow of our number three cellist flying over the instrument. No problems for her. For me it is a wild scramble. It is hard for me even to make my *eyes* move fast enough across the lines of notes, let alone play those notes. My mind is full of frantic thoughts. Here come some quarter notes, I can play *them* at least. But now a strange-looking passage. Are these octaves? How in the world do I finger this section? How do I play it when I don't even know what it sounds like? Ah, three measures of rest. At least I can count this, one-two-three-four, one-two-three-four, one-two-three-four, play! Oops! Too soon; I am a beat ahead of the cellists in front of me. How in the world could I have miscounted those measures of rest? Could *they* have made a mistake? No. No time to worry about it; here come a bunch of sixteenth notes. I'll never make them at this tempo. Try to catch the first note in each group of four, the way they all tell you. That's a lot easier said than done. Damn! I've lost my place. How come those guys can read this stuff right off the paper? I'll try to catch the other cellists when they come out of this passage. There! Back with them again. Out of the corner of my eye I see that my partner has lost his place. With left index finger I point it out to him on the music, moving the finger along for a measure or two until he gets the swing of it. Now an easy, exposed passage for us, a chance to make some nice sounds. Oops! I'm not with the folks in front. What happened? No time now to think about it. What in the world is this coming up? Try to imitate what the people in front are playing. *Look* at the notes, don't skim them, *don't give up.* Lost my place again, can't tell where the others are. Look ahead, there's some low notes, watch them, see when their bows go down to the C string. There! Now! Back with them for a while anyway. Whew! The conductor is stopping, wants to do something again. Quick look at that bad passage, how can I finger that? No time, here we go again, have to work that out at home.

And so until break, five minutes or so, and then on until 9:25, when we stop. We pack up stands, music, instruments, talking and gossiping a little more freely after playing. I feel full of excitement and tension, the way I used to, years ago, after playing a close and fast game of Ping-Pong—it always took me an hour or so to wind down. The leaders of the orchestra do their best to break up our little gossip sessions: "Come on, everybody, we're supposed to be out of here by now." Someone offers me a ride to the Square. Once there, I go down into the subway, take the train back to Charles Street, walk home. Twenty past ten. Still time for a little practice before I go to bed. Let's take a look at that hard passage, work it out with a metronome. An hour later I am playing it—at just half the proper tempo. Enough for today.

Monday

9

Tuesday

Tuesday is quartet day. Three other amateurs and I meet once a week to play under a professional coach. I take my cello and musical stuff to my office. In the morning, an hour or so before time to leave, I set up my music, tune up, warm up, and play a number of times whatever music we are going to work on. This is one of the fringe benefits of being self-employed—you can play music in your own office. When the time comes, I pack everything up again and take the subway to Park Street station. It is always crowded; I can't help bumping into people with the cello. Change at Park Street for the line to Harvard Square, again crowded. There I wait for my violinist friend to pick me up in her car. As we drive up to the small school where we play, we exchange news and small talk. In a small practice room we set up our stands and music. I tune my A string to a tuning fork, the others tune their A strings to mine. Quite often our coach has us warm up, and tune up our ears, by playing a scale or two in various ways, or certain chords, or now and then a Bach chorale which she has written out for string quartet. Then we start work on our main piece.

It is an early Mozart quartet, in C, K.157 (the K standing for Köchel, who made a catalogue of all Mozart's music). It is a lovely piece, which we are going to play in a few weeks at a small recital. It takes about eleven or so minutes to play, at the tempi at which we play it, and we have been working on it for months, a movement at a time, often a part of a movement at a time. Today we begin at the beginning. The first movement begins with the main theme, a simple little tune, one of the most perfect, swinging tunes ever written. We play it through once softly, then back a second time, this time loud and strong. We have done it about fifty times, and just as it did the first time, it makes the back of my neck prickle. But something soon goes wrong; the coach stops us, talks about the music, we start again. Before long we stop once more. We are not exactly together in rhythm, or we are playing too loud, or too heavily, or have speeded up, or an important part is not being heard, or we are not in tune. The coach makes a correction, we go back a few bars, try again. Not right yet. We stop, try again. Better this time. We play on, until we hit another rough spot, stop, talk about it, play it again, and then again. We skip to other places in the movement where we have had trouble, or where, even if we are playing correctly, we are not playing elegantly or musically.

We move on to the second movement, *andante*—which means going along, an easy walking pace. What a nice surprise it was, in Italy, to find out that musical terms meant something outside of music. *Allegro* means gay, energetic, in good spirits, *"Piano, piano"* means, "Take it easy, don't get upset." A *scherzo* is a joke. The bus stops at the *fermata.* And so on. This andante of Mozart's is completely different in character from the first movement—gentle, reflective, melancholy. It begins with one of the most heartbreakingly beautiful tunes ever written. I have heard it fifty times, and each time I hear it it makes my eyes sting. Listening to this I wait for my entrance, come in, nice easy notes. But even in this early Mozart quartet nothing is easy for long. Soon I have some sixteenth notes to play, in eight groups of five. On paper they look easy; for a violin, they would be. But there is no easy and at the same time musical way to play them on a cello. The best fingering I could work out still requires a very awkward, left-hand stretch; for months I have been doing exercises with that hand so that I could play these notes. I play them now; not bad, but still not quite right; it should *sound* easy, even if it isn't.

The quartet is (for me) less tense than the orchestra, but much more intense. In the orchestra I am drowned out by many better players. I struggle hard to catch what notes I can, but nobody hears, knows, or cares whether I catch them or not.

Tuesday

11

In the quartet I have much easier notes, but they are mine alone, and I have to get them right—at the right time, at the right loudness, for the right length, and above all, *exactly* in tune. It takes a different kind of concentration. Often we play a few bars of music over and over again, six, ten times, trying to get it right. We play one note, and hold it, to get a chord in tune. Or we play a passage two players at a time, so we can hear and feel how our parts sound together. The two violins play together; then viola and cello. Then all four of us play the passage, two, three times. Then we fit it into the whole movement. Sometimes I have one or two notes to play, over and over. Sometimes I just wait and listen (meanwhile stretching that left hand), while the others work out a problem in their parts. It is slow work. We progress by inches. Once in a great while I feel we are trampling over ground we have walked on many times, and wish we could play more music. But most of the time I find both interesting and exciting our efforts to perfect, as far as we can, this simple but (like all Mozart) subtle quartet. All the time, as we work, we know that before long we will play this quartet for an audience—a very small audience, but an audience of people who *know,* and who will hear (even if they forgive) our every fault and mistake. We can hear our playing of the piece getting better. But will it be good? Will we be able to do before other people what we have learned to do in practice—where, after all, if you make a mistake or get mixed up you can always go back and start again?

We play for an hour and a half. Then we pack up again, my violinist friend drives me to the Square, and I take the subway home. There I spend some time building into my nervous system whatever we worked on that day, and also practicing those groups of sixteenths. That done, I begin to get musically ready for Thursday.

A Week of Music

Thursday

About midday on Thursday I again take the subway from my office to Harvard Square, where again my violinist friend picks me up in her car. This time we drive to the house of a friend, the pianist in our piano trio. We set up in the living room, tune, and begin. Often we warm up with a Haydn trio; the violinist and pianist read off their harder parts, while I struggle with my easier ones. Then we turn to our main work, the Mendelssohn Trio in D minor. It is an extraordinarily beautiful piece, one the great piano trios, full of lovely tunes, beautifully fitted together, with all three players getting wonderful things to play. It is also much too hard for us. We have struggled for months to learn to play it. Today we begin with the first movement, which we have worked on most and know best. Against a discreet rhythmic background from the piano, I play the main theme, a lovely, broad, flowing tune. It is tempting to take my tempo from the piano, but I mustn't; I have to play with conviction, and let the piano take the tempo from me. I try not to go too fast; I know that the excitement of the music is going to make us speed up later. The notes of my part lie right where my cello makes what they call "wolf notes," notes that tend to skip up one octave, like a Swiss yodeler or a boy whose voice is changing. It is hard to play them clearly yet not too loud or too roughly.

For a minute or two all goes well, and we swing along; then there is trouble. At the end of a passage which I and the violin are supposed to finish together, she is finishing a beat ahead of me. We stop. We play it again; same result. Once again, same result. I think I may be coming in too late; we play it more slowly, I count very carefully, I can tell that I have come in right. But by the end of the passage I am behind again. We have played this part correctly before; what has happened? We look at our scores. The violin is sure she is right, I am sure that I am. A coach could tell us in a second what is wrong, but we have no coach, and have to puzzle it out for ourselves. Thinking that the violin may be counting wrongly somewhere in her part, I ask her to play, while I follow in the score. She does, and I can see that she is right, and say so. She plays it once again, while I hum my part, seeing how her notes and mine fit together. And now I find the trouble; there are two eighth note rests in my part, and for some reason I have taken to playing them, and worse yet, *hearing* them, as quarter note rests. I apologize to my colleagues, thinking to myself, "How in the world did I come to do that?" We play the section again, and this time it comes out right. And in some way having found our, in this case my, mistake, is more satisfying than it would have been had a coach pointed it out.

We play on. At one point, after some measures of rest, I enter with the second big tune of the movement. I have listened to the record, and studied the score, and know that I come in about a measure after there is a change in the harmony of the piano part. But that change, which I hear very clearly on the record, I can't hear now, and I miss my entrance. We go back and do it again—same result. I decide to count my measures of rest carefully, instead of listening for the piano cue. But the piano part is thick with notes, and I don't hear the beat clearly enough, so that again we are not quite together. We work on it some more, it gets better, we decide to keep going. Soon we come to what is perhaps the most beautiful part of this very beautiful movement. The piano plays some descending chords in strange harmonies, the violin and I play some very soft octaves, and then I play once again, as softly as I dare (those wolf notes!) the opening tune, while the violin plays a lovely accompaniment. This part makes our eyes sting every time we play it, and mine every time I hear it. But we sometimes have trouble fitting our entrances together, and today we have to play it several times to get it right.

In the second movement, which is on the whole the easiest, there is one bit that is rhythmically very tricky. The violin and I have a number of bars to play in which we must play two notes, or count two beats, to the piano's three. We keep wanting to speed up our notes to match the piano's, in which case we get ahead of the piano. We do this over and over. We all look at our scores, trying to get a sense of how this ought to sound. Finally the violin and I decide that once we set our rhythm we have to shut our ears and our minds to the piano, play as if it were not there—which is hard, since the piano is meant to be heard. We try to lock ourselves into our rhythm by bobbing our heads and shoulders up and down as we play. Finally, after many tries, we get it right. We stop and applaud each other. (Later I listen to my recording of this trio, played by the Beaux Arts Trio, perhaps the finest piano trio now playing. Even their violin and cello can't wholly resist the temptation to speed up during this section, but the piano adjusts, so that they come out even.)

We try the third movement, a scherzo, light and quick as a hummingbird. The piano begins, and after some measures the violin and I come in with very light staccato notes. It is a hard entrance to count, even going at two-thirds speed. The violin keeps missing her entrance by a fraction of a beat. We look at the music, and work it out that we come in after the piano has played five rising three-note figures. We hear in our minds how it goes, try it; it works. Later the violin has a descending figure of several bars, which I then echo. I don't get the entrance right. We try again; still not right. Once more we turn to the scores—when you work with a coach, the coach has the score and *tells* you what to do—and figure out how my notes follow hers. In teeny little notes, in red pencil, I write her closing notes on my part, to help my memory. We play it again,

Thursday

15

and it works. And so, through the movement, we hunt down and correct mistakes as we make them, until two hours or more have gone by (like minutes) and it is time to go home.

Practice

On other days I practice. I study my orchestra, quartet, and trio parts, work out fingerings—which fingers of my left hand shall I use to hold down the strings?—and bowings. I take a passage that is hard for me to play, and play it in strict time against a metronome. I pick a tempo, no matter how slow, at which I can play it. Then I speed up the metronome a notch or two and play it again. When I have it in my fingers, I speed up a bit more and try again. At some point my fingers begin to trip and stumble. I feel myself growing tense, stop, let my arms hang limp by my sides for a second or two, then start again. Sometimes it may be only two or three notes that are the hardest to play. I play those three notes again and again, until I can play them clearly, then speed up some more. Sometimes, to get the feeling of speed into my brain and fingers, instead of playing each one of those notes singly, I will play them in groups of three or four, that is, the first note three (or four) times, then the next note three (or four) times, and so on. Then try them again one at a time. Then play the entire passage the notes came from. Sooner or later I hit a barrier; no matter how hard I try, or how many tricks I think up, I am not going to play those particular notes faster on this particular day.

So I turn to something else. I may work on trills, again with the metronome, trilling second finger against first, or third against second, or (hardest of all) fourth against third. I may play scales, or octaves. I may play successive intervals—a second, third, a fourth—up and down the A string, or an exercise of my own invention in which I go up, say, a fifth, then down a fourth, and so on up the string. Or I may try, with eyes closed, to play all the possible A's (or B's, C's, etc.) on the fingerboard. Or I may do some left-hand, double-stop exercises (in which I hold one string down with one finger and another down with another) from Janos Starker's book. Some of these stretches my fingers won't make; like a gymnast, or a dancer at the barre, I use my right hand now and then to stretch the fingers of my left. Or I may play scales, two, three, or four octaves, or arpeggios; or any one of a number of exercises in my exercise book. Or I may do some left-hand exercises I invented, or some exercises in the thumb position. I work with one set of muscles until they begin to feel tired, then switch to another set. I work on vibrato, often holding my left thumb clear of the neck of the cello, to avoid any temptation to press with it.

Since I am a poor sight reader, I try to take time at almost every practice to sight-read new music—the cello parts of the Mozart or Haydn quartets, or the Beethoven trios, quartets, or sonatas. Or I may play again a piece I once worked on, but haven't played for a long time—the Brahms E-minor Sonata, or the Clarinet Trio in A minor, or other movements of the Bach suites or sonatas, or other quartets. Once in a great while —this is often a good project for summer, when I am under less pressure to practice a work I am playing with a group— I may spend hours puzzling out a great work that is a hundred times too hard for me, like the Haydn or Dvořák concertos. Every year I take a new look at the Dvořák, and am encouraged; passages that once took me many hours to work out (and that a good player plays in a minute or two) I now may work out in an hour or less. Each new time around, those notes look a little less mysterious, a little more meaningful. And it makes hearing the work much more fun; in sections that once seemed just a blur of notes, I now hear every note, because I have slowly found those notes, one by one.

Sometimes, when my hands get tired and need a rest, I will

take a piece I am learning, set the metronome at a much faster speed than I could ever play it, and see if at that speed I can sing or hum, or hear in my mind, the music. If the eye can follow it and the brain hear it at the proper speed, there is a chance that the fingers may keep up; if the eye and brain are also confused, there is no chance. Sometimes I put the score of a work, like the Mendelssohn trio, on the stand and play the recording, following with my eyes, as I listen, not only my part, but the violin and piano parts as well. If I do this enough, I can look at the score (without the recording) and hear in memory what the other instruments were doing at that point. Or I can play my own part from the score, and at the same time hear in my mind what the others would be doing. Sometimes I take unfamiliar music and just read it for rhythm, humming tunelessly dum-dum-dum-ta-tiddle-um, so that I become more able to recognize rhythmic patterns at sight. I may do this with the metronome, speeding up the tempo faster and faster.

There is much to do, much more to do than I can ever find time for. Each time I begin to practice, I think to myself, "Today I will work on this, this, this, and this." I always run out of time long before these projects are completed. Or my hands get tired, or my mind—reading new music, even if only for rhythm, is very intensive and demanding work; an hour of it is about as much as I can do at a time.

How did this all begin?

2

Early Music Memories

Family

During my growing up there was very little music in my family; some on my mother's side, on my father's side none at all. I have been told that when my father's mother was young, she studied music, played the piano, and was a fine singer; that two of my father's sisters were also good singers; and that when the children were growing up in Grand Rapids, Michigan, the family often went to hear concerts of visiting musicians. But by the time I was a child whatever interest in music there had been in my father's family had died out. In the years I knew her, my grandmother was quite deaf, and wore a hearing aid; this may have had something to do with it. At any rate, I was very close to my father's parents, visited them in Grand Rapids almost every summer until my grandfather died when I was about fourteen, spent Christmas with them when I was about eight, and visited them for an entire and wonderfully happy winter when I was eleven. In all that time I never saw or heard even a hint of their former interest in music. In their big house there was no piano or any other musical instrument. In the upstairs hall was a big old wind-up Victrola, but it did not work, and in any case there were no records to play on it. They had an old arch-shaped radio at one end of the big living room, which they used to listen to once in a while. In my mind's eye I can see them sitting beside it, listening intently, but I can't remember what they were listening to; perhaps news, or commentators, but not music. Except for my grandfather's whistle, about which more a little later, I can't remember ever hearing either of them sing, or hum, or whistle, even a fragment of a song. We talked about many things. They could talk to me without talking down to me or making me feel that because I was little my thoughts had no importance. But I do not remember ever talking, or hearing any talk, about music.

My father had two brothers and three sisters. As with my grandparents, in all the years I knew them I never heard any of them sing, hum, or whistle, any part of a song or tune. Once or twice I heard my father sing a few notes, but only to show that he couldn't. And I may have once heard my Uncle Tom do the same. My Aunt Belle married a man who loved music, the painter Randall Davey, who took up the cello in his fifties and became quite a good player. In his house in Santa Fe he often played classical records; he gave me my first recording of David Oistrakh, and introduced me to the music of Vivaldi. My Uncle John married a woman who loved music and knew something about it, but I don't think much of this rubbed off on him or my cousins.

My mother's family was somewhat more musical. Her parents were divorced before I was born. When we were very little we spent our summers near Grandfather Crocker. I remember him as a very jovial and energetic man with beautiful cars and a big sailboat. From the age of seven or eight on, I saw very little of him. I have no musical memories of him; how musical he may have been, I just don't know. My sisters and I saw a great deal of Granny, and were very close to her during our growing up. She was a devout Episcopalian and went regularly to church on Sunday, taking us with her, which we half disliked and half enjoyed. Like all little children we were bored in church, which made no sense and seemed to go on forever. But it was obviously a serious grown-up occasion, and it was an important part of our lives with Granny. Anyway, we knew that a wonderful Sunday lunch would follow, which kept us going. In church Granny, whose speaking voice was quite low, sang the hymns in a strong, clear, tremulous soprano. It embarrassed me terribly because it was so loud, and even more because it was so emotional. I felt sure that the whole church must be staring at us. Much later in life I would realize what marvelous songs those old hymns were, and even though I did not believe much of what they said, would enjoy singing them out.

Granny used to go to orchestra concerts from time to time with an old and dear friend, who had a box at Carnegie Hall. But I do not remember that she ever had any classical records, and can't recall ever hearing any classical music in her house, or, later, in her New York apartment. Certainly music was not a big part of her life; she was more interested in books and theatre. But it was at least a part.

My mother must have studied piano when she was young. My sister remembers her playing a few pieces, usually at parties. I only remember her playing one small fragment, but what I can recall of the way she played it suggests that when young she must have played fairly well. She had a very true and discerning ear. Late in her life, when she and my father moved to a retirement hotel in La Jolla, California, she began to go into San Diego quite regularly to concerts of both the San Diego Symphony and the Los Angeles Philharmonic. She sent me reviews of many of the concerts written by what she called "the crosspatch critic" of the San Diego paper, and usually added her own perceptive and witty comments. One of the last things we did together was to go to a concert of the San Diego Symphony, where we heard Liadov's *Kikimora,* Ravel's *Shéhérazade,* and Mahler's Fourth Symphony. I looked forward to going to other concerts with her, and to sharing in other ways our mutual love of music, but soon after that she became very ill and died a few months later.

Whatever musical interest or talent she may have had, she showed no signs of it during our growing up. There was no music in our house. My sister and I discovered, in a garage or basement or somewhere, an old wind-up Victrola and some records of old songs which we used to play from time to time. But we never heard it played by anyone else. We had a radio, but my parents rarely listened to it, and almost never to any kind of music. I do have one odd fragment of memory of my mother hearing on the radio a brand-new singer named Bing Crosby, and saying that if he could just get the huskiness out of his voice he might be quite a success. I never heard her sing or hum a tune.

In our house we had a kind of mini-upright piano, with a keyboard of only sixty or seventy keys. Most of the time the only person who used it was my younger sister, who was made to take piano lessons and to practice. There was one tune in her practice book called "The Happy Farmer," which she played for what seemed like hours. In time her reluctance, her lack of progress, and perhaps most of all "The Happy Farmer," wore my parents down and the lessons and practice stopped. Later, at school, she took up the bugle and played for a while in a drum-and-bugle corps. She had a natural lip and a powerful tone. Some years later, just after she was married, I went with her to a formal dance. During an intermission she asked the trumpet player in the band if she could try out his trumpet. He smiled indulgently and handed it over. She wiped off her lipstick, set her lips, took a deep breath, and blew a tremendous blast. A more surprised man I never saw.

My mother hardly ever touched the piano. I remember her playing only one piece. At college my father had been on the football team, had joined the best clubs, and all that. It had been a high point in his life. One of our family rituals was to go to several football games each fall, eating a picnic lunch before the game with my father's college classmates and their families. My mother, like all football wives, went along with this. Only many years later did I begin to sense or guess that (like many other wives) she may have felt all this football, cheering, and nostalgia was a lot of nonsense.

At any rate, once in a great while she would sit down at the tiny piano and play the first line or two of my father's college football song, the one the band played when the football team first appeared on the field. She played it in time and in tune, but somehow it sounded very different, and all wrong, in a way I could not quite put my finger on. One of the things she did was to arpeggiate the chords in the bass, playing the notes separately instead of together, which gave a somewhat tinkly effect. Hearing her now in my mind, I can see that she was making fun of the song, changing it from a stirring march into something that a teacher might play in a kindergarten or nursery school as the children marched around the room. Her mockery and wit were far too subtle for my father; hearing the start of the song that all his life, and like no other, made his heart beat faster and the blood surge in his veins, he would urge her to keep on playing. No, she would say, that's enough. And that is all I ever heard her sing or play.

I Can't Carry a Tune

My father used to say very often how much he loved music. I remember being told that when I was very small I could make him cry by singing "Londonderry Air." ("O Danny Boy, the pipes, the pipes are play-ay-ing.") But my father could not sing. He used to say that he wished he could, as an amputee might say he wished he could have his missing arm or leg back. But, he would go on to say sadly, though he had tried his best, he had never been able to carry a tune. At college he had been the manager of the glee club, and had traveled with them and enjoyed their singing. But he had never been able to take part.

I can remember, perhaps two or three times during my growing up, hearing him try to sing a few notes. The occasion was always a party, with some of his old friends around. After everyone had had a few drinks and was feeling mellow, the subject might turn to music, and someone would suggest that my father sing them a tune. Come on, Harry, sing us something! No, you know I can't sing. Sure you can, sure you can, don't be shy. No, I can't, I can't carry a tune. Oh come on, give it a try. As I think of it now, it seems very much like the little drama enacted every fall in the comic strip *Peanuts*, when Lucy tries once again to persuade Charlie Brown to place-kick a football which she offers to hold for him, promising this time not to pull it away at the last second as she has always done in years past. Eventually, after much cajoling and reassuring, my father would be persuaded. What song shall I sing, I don't know any songs. In time, a song would be decided on. The party would be summoned to silence, and my father would begin to sing. He was rarely able to get out more than four or five notes before the crowd would burst into roars of laughter. My father would stop, and with some mixture of embarrassment and pleasure join in the laughter against himself. In one way, he may not have liked it; in another, it made him the center of attention, it was his parlor trick. The idea that he could not sing was not just a part, but a treasured part, of his notion of himself.

Many years later I would read, in a very important and little known book, *Self-Consistency*, by the unjustly neglected psychologist Prescott Lecky, that people cling to and protect their images of themselves even when these images contain faults, weaknesses, incapacities. Thus, in a study of Columbia University students who were poor spellers, he discovered to his great surprise that many of them, though they said they were ashamed of not being able to spell, were in fact in a strange way proud of it. At any rate, they were more interested in defending their image of themselves as nonspellers than they were in learning how to spell. Years later I saw this in many children in school and called it the protective strategy of deliberate failure. It is easier to say, "I'm a nonspeller (or a nonsinger)" than to face the risks and possible disappointments of learning to sing or spell.

Every so often my mother used to tease my father about his singing. When she teased, it was not for fun; she meant it to hurt, and it usually did. She was very perceptive, with a sure eye for other people's weaknesses and soft spots; she knew just where to stick the needle to make it hurt most. In the case of my father's singing, she would refer now and then, with the light and mocking lilt she could put in her voice, to an obscure song called "All The Little Pansy Faces." Though I never asked about this and she never told me, I gather that at some point early in their life, at some sort of gathering, my father had tried to sing this sentimental little song, which he perhaps liked very much. The results must not have been good. When she mentioned the pansy faces, his face made it clear that this was not a happy memory.

I went along with my father's and everyone else's idea of him as a nonsinger. Not until many years after I was grown up did I get a hint that it might never have been true. Once again he was prevailed on to sing a song, and once again, after just a few words, he was stopped by everyone's laughter. But this time he was singing a song I happened to know, and listening carefully I discovered to my surprise that he sang it quite well, that if

I Can't Carry a Tune

not dead on the tune he was very close to it. He was in fact much less of a so-called monotone than a student of mine whom I later taught to sing well. All of which makes me wonder, at what point in his life, and in what way, did someone —a friend? a relative? a teacher? a music teacher?—and perhaps with the best of intentions, slam the doors to music in my father's face?

This happens every year to tens of thousands of children, perhaps at home, more likely in school. The children are told to sing a song. Some child does not get it quite right. Perhaps the other children laugh, or some child—I have known a few like this—says, "Teacher, he isn't singing it right," or the teacher himself points it out. Before long there is a suggestion made that when the class is singing, particularly before outsiders (above all, parents), this child sing very softly. The child gets the idea. Something about his not being able to sing goes into his school record, so that later teachers will be alerted. And so the story is passed on.

My Grandfather's Whistle

The only other musical sound I can remember being made by anyone on my father's side of the family was a little tune that my grandfather used to whistle to himself. As he was about seventy when I was born, I knew him only as an old man. But he was a sweet man, a lovely man, and his kindness and love and friendship were a great joy and comfort to me in my growing up. He was tall and very handsome, with white hair and moustache. He was born and brought up on a farm in Paris, in Bourbon County, Kentucky, and looked like a sort of idealized Southern gentleman in a whiskey ad, but wiser, stronger, and kinder. (He would never have let himself be used for such a purpose.) He lived for much of his life, and all the time I knew him, in a big, rather ugly (but lovely to me) Victorian house in Grand Rapids, Michigan. When he got up in the morning, or came home from the office at midday for lunch, or in the evening, and opened the big front door of the house (whose sound I still remember) and came into the front hall, he would very often whistle a little tune, which went about like this:

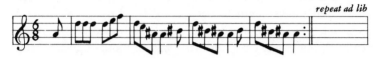

The notes are only approximate. They are not meant to suggest that he whistled his little tune strictly in tune, and always the same. The tune was faintly tuneless, and the melody would sometimes sag downwards a tone or so near the end. Sometimes, but by no means always, he would follow it with something like this—the notes, again, very approximate:

These two notes very flexible in pitch.

How I loved the sound of that whistle, and love the memory of it! But it was the only tune or song I ever heard in all the years I was a happy visitor in that house.

First Concert

When I was about eight or nine, my sisters and I all caught whooping cough. I caught it first, a fairly mild case. As I was recovering, they both came down with it and became very sick. Since the house was in a turmoil, I went for a few weeks to live with Granny in her New York apartment. While I was there a good friend of hers invited us to go to a concert of the New York Philharmonic in Carnegie Hall. I was eager to go, but though I was no longer sick or contagious, as an aftereffect of the disease I still had a persistent tickling cough. But Granny was determined to take me to the concert. She knew that since my parents never went to concerts, if I did not go with her I was not likely to go at all. She may have hoped that I would enjoy it, but in any case, and what was far more important, she thought such exposure would be good for me. As far as the cough went, she was a great believer in will power. If I made up my mind that I would not cough, I would not feel any need to cough. She was a kind but, to an eight-year-old, quite formidable woman. When she bent her eaglelike gaze upon me and told me that no matter what, I was *Not to Cough,* I got the message. To help will power a little, she gave me a box of Allenbury's Black Currant Pastilles, and told me to keep sucking—noiselessly—on one of them.

Thus warned, armed, and prepared, I arrived at the concert. Our seats, as I very dimly recall, were in a box, on the left side, quite close to the stage. The hall was a dazzle. I had never seen such a huge room so full of people. Everything was strange, meaningless, fascinating. All those people on the stage, all those strange sounds. But for that cough, the concert might well have been a delight for me. Instead it was an agony. To fight back a cough is hard enough (or too hard) even for adults, as any concertgoer knows. For a child it was close to torture. How much of the time I was actually fighting back a cough, and how much of the time I was worrying that I might have to, I don't remember. I felt Granny's eye on me all the while. My visible struggles not to cough may well have spoiled the concert for her, as well as me.

Early Music Memories

In later years she took me and my sister Jane to the theater many times. These were always happy occasions. But I did not go to another symphony concert (and then not with her) until my mid-twenties, when I had left the Navy and was living and working in New York.

My First Instrument

When I was about nine or ten someone gave me for Christmas an instrument called a banjo-ukulele. This was a hybrid—strung, tuned, and played like a ukulele, but with a banjolike head, on which someone had painted some sort of Hawaiian scene. At first I was excited with my new toy. Two of my friends had ukuleles, or ukes, of the ordinary kind, with a wooden body. From them, or an instruction book, I learned to tune the instrument to the notes of the scale sol-do-mi-la, to which we sang a little song, "My Dog Has Fleas." From these friends, or perhaps the book, I learned to sing "Little Brown Jug," strumming an accompaniment of three or four chords. It seemed a good trick, and like all kids with a new trick, I was happy to do it for a while. But after that, what else was there to do? We didn't know anybody else who played the ukulele. It didn't make a pretty enough sound to make us want to play it more. We didn't know any good songs that we wanted to sing, and in fact, didn't want to sing at all.

What we really wanted to do, and did, was make model airplanes; along with *playing* football and baseball—we had not yet become fans—it was the central passion of our lives. It was real work and, in a small way, real craftsmanship. In those days there were no molded plastic parts, all made and ready to glue together. What we bought were kits—Ideal Model Airplanes, in orange boxes, and for a quarter(!)—which contained a block of balsa wood for the fuselage, a small flat piece of balsa for the wings and tail, some bamboo strips for wing and wheel struts, two wheels, a bit of sandpaper, some glue, a couple of tiny bottles of colored paint (irresistibly beguiling to my destructive little sister), and some simple plans. From these plans we traced onto the balsa wood the outlines of wings, tail, and fuselage. With single-edged razor blades, or maybe sharp pocket knives, we then cut out these parts, lovingly sandpapered them to the proper aerodynamic shapes, then glued them together—also delicate work—and painted them. We usually did this together, and as we worked and talked, enjoyed a rich fantasy life in these mostly World War I airplanes, though for some of the newer airplanes we invented new and even more exotic wars. My own favorite plane was the Curtis Akron Fighter, a small biplane designed to be launched from and recovered by large airships. It seemed the most beautiful object I had ever seen; just to look at a picture of the plane, or at the plans, or even at one of my own models of it, gave me a thrill of pleasure. I *loved* that airplane, and much of my fantasy life revolved around it.

Compared to all this, what was "Little Brown Jug" or the banjo-uke? In a short while it went into a closet. Whether my parents gave it away or threw it away, I don't know. I never missed it, never looked for it, never thought about it again.

Remembered Songs

Among my musical memories are some songs of the late twenties and early thirties. Good songs, with lyrics usually sexist by today's standards, often ridiculously sentimental, but often wonderfully lighthearted and foolish.

> Yes, sir, that's my baby
> No, sir, don't mean maybe
> Yes, sir, that's my baby now

You're the cream in my coffee,
You're the lace in my shoe,
You will always be,
My necessity,
I'd be lost without you.

Then there was "The Million Dollar Baby in the Five-and-Ten-Cent Store," "You're My Everything," from an Ed Wynn show, a couple of sentimental ones, "Just a Gigolo," and "The Boulevard of Broken Dreams," and one I remember especially fondly:

Step up all you gentlemen
Lift your toppers high [or, blimey but you're shy]
Say hello to the Duchess.
Hiya Duchess old pal, old kid, old sock,
old thing, old gal.

One song, or rather, something in the instrumental background of the song, made a great impression on me. The song was "Mad About The Boy" (by Noel Coward), the recording by Ray Noble and his orchestra. The music began with a rhythmic pattern of five notes, what musicians call (I later learned) an *ostinato* ("obstinate"), played over and over again. On tuned tympani? Bass fiddle? Piano? Some combination of these? I couldn't tell. That rhythmic figure stuck fast in my memory; over the years it has played itself many times in my mind. Only when I started this book did I begin to try to figure out what the notes were. They proved to be very simple: the first five notes of the major scale played backwards, thus: G F E D C, or sol-fa-mi-re-do, but with the fourth note, the D or "re," flatted or lowered another half-step, to D flat or C sharp. These notes were played to the rhythm dum, dum, dum-da-dum, or

Something about that insistent rhythmic pattern, the first ostinato I had ever heard, or about the descending notes, or the sound, slightly sinister, of that flatted fourth note, all caught my musical imagination.

Good songs all, sung in the style of the times by men with rather high, swoony voices. When we moved from New York City to New Canaan, we began to listen to the radio, from which I picked up a few more songs. There was only one program we really cared about—"Buck Rogers, in the Twenty-Fifth *Cen*-tury!" We lived for it, and in it. It came on at 6 P.M., and we never knew until the last minute whether we would be able to listen to it or not. If my father took the early train home from work, he would arrive just as the program started, and he always made us turn it off. If he took the later train, he didn't get home until the program was over—and there was nothing after it that we cared about hearing. Naturally we always pulled for that later train. Buck Rogers had no songs or music, but there were songs on other programs that came just before it, that we listened to from time to time. There was the football song of Hudson High, from the program "Jack Armstrong, the All-American Boy":

> Wave the flag for Hudson High, boys
> Show them how we stand
> Ever shall our team be champions
> Known throughout the land (Rah! Rah!)

At about 4:45 a trio of singers, Brook, Dave, and Bunny came on, sponsored by the soap Oxol:

Early Music Memories

32

It beats all, how Oxol, just cleans all it touches
And makes each wash as white as winter snow.

Then there was a program "Bobby Benson—Sunny Jim—
and *Windy!*" We only listened to the end of it because it came
on just before Buck Rogers, and we didn't want to miss a
second of that. So we got to know the Bobby Benson closing
song. To this day I don't know whether it was, so to speak, a
real song, or one written just for the program. But I liked it
then and do now:

Goin' back, to my good old Texas home, home, home
Down by the sleepy Rio Grande
Where the lonesome turtle does his grievin'
And the moonbeams shine down on the sand.
Goin' back, where the longhorn cattle roam, roam, roam
And your best friend is your bronco and your gun (ya-hoo!)
There I know I'll never more be leavin'
Texas home my ramblin' days are done.

Then there was the awful Li'l Orphan Annie song. We
despised Li'l Orphan Annie. Come to think about it, we didn't
like any programs—or for that matter, any books—that were
about children. In our fantasy lives we were always grown-ups.
But even though we didn't like Li'l Orphan Annie or her song
either, the song stuck in my mind.

We also learned the New Canaan High School football song:

Onward, New Canaan
Fight to the end!
Raise high the red and black
Our name to defend, etc.

Like most high school football songs it was probably lifted
from some college song, but I don't know which one.

Remembered Songs
———   ———

33

In seventh grade I had the only music class in my entire school career. It was nothing we looked forward to. A young man taught us. Did we sing? I suppose so, but I forget what. What else did we do? I have no idea.

Jolly Boating Weather

It was during these years that, for the first time in my life, I was strongly moved by a piece of music. It happened at Granny's house in Falmouth Foreside, just outside of Portland, Maine, where we used to visit every summer. In the summers when I was about eight or nine, Granny's sister Aunt Jessie came to visit her. In an already happy summer, this was always an especially happy occasion. Children always like visitors (since we felt that Granny's house was *our* house, we felt that Aunt Jessie was visiting *us*). New adults are interesting, if they are kindly and friendly, as Aunt Jessie was. Visitors change the routine of the house, stir up things a bit. Also, though we loved Granny and felt comfortable around her, she was a rather serious and austere woman, while Aunt Jessie was more informal, more of a joker. The two women liked to talk and had much to talk about. Like all serious adult talk this was very interesting to us children.

But perhaps Aunt Jessie's greatest attraction for us was that she could play the piano, the first person we had ever known who could really play any musical instrument. On many evenings we would all go into a small sitting room, Aunt Jessie would sit down at the large black upright piano, and we would play and sing together songs from a book called *College Songs*. It was a large, old book, probably published well before the turn of the century. Of the songs we sang, I have since heard only two. One was called "Upidee," the words taken from the poem

"Excelsior" about the youth who for reasons not made clear carried a "banner with a strange device" to the top of an Alp where he froze to death. After each verse of the original poem, this nonsense chorus:

> Upidee, idee, ida
> Upidee, upida
> Upidee, idee, ida
> Upidee ida

A sad poem (perhaps) but a merry song. The other was called "Funiculi, funicula." It may have been taken from a Neapolitan song; many years later I would hear it as one of the main themes of Richard Strauss's tone poem "Aus Italien."

Wonderful, tuneful, spirited songs.

There were two songs that we often sang at the same time, my first taste of polyphony. One was "The Spanish Cavalier," the other "Solomon Levi." There was always much discussion about who would sing "Solomon Levi" and who would sing "The Spanish Cavalier." The melody of the "Spanish Cavalier" went higher, and there were fewer words, so more chance to let loose with a ringing tone. But "Solomon Levi" had more interesting words, and it was a musical challenge to see if we could keep them in time with the other song. I think Granny and Jane may have sung the "Cavalier," while Aunt Jessie and I collaborated on "Solomon Levi."

One of the best of them all was "Michael Roy." From time to time I have sung this song to people who know many old American songs, but I have yet to meet anyone who has ever even heard of it. Because it is too good to be lost, I am going to put down here both the words and the music. I hope some readers will try it out:

Jolly Boating Weather

35

In Brooklyn city there lived a maid
And she was known to fame
Her mother's name was Mary Ann
And hers was Mary Jane
And every Saturday morning
She used to go over the river
And went to the market where she sold eggs
And sausages, likewise liver.

chorus

For-oh, for-oh, for he was my darling boy
Oh, he was the lad with the auburn hair
And his name was Michael Roy

She fell in love with a charcoal lad
McCloskey was his name
His fighting weight was seven stone ten
And he loved sweet Mary Jane
He took her to ride in his donkey cart
On a fine St. Patrick's Day
But the donkey took fright at a Jersey man
And started to run away

chorus

McCloskey shouted and hollered in vain
But the donkey wouldn't stop
He threw Mary Jane right over its head
And into a crockery shop
But when he saw this awful sight
His heart was moved with pity
So he stabbed the donkey with a bit of charcoal
And started for Salt Lake City

chorus

Jolly Boating Weather

37

But the song that gave me what I might call my first aesthetic experience, one of being strongly moved by something in the music itself, was called "Jolly Boating Weather." A note told us that it was the Eton boating song. I didn't know what or where Eton was, thought the boats were sailboats, and didn't know what a "stein" was. But every time we sang the song, it made my eyes water and my throat choke up.

The song began like this: (I include what words I can remember)

The first three lines are ordinary enough, pleasant but nothing exceptional. It was in the fourth line that the music took the turn that always surprised and moved me. One might have expected the fourth line to go something like this:

or perhaps this:

But instead, it did this:

Just as it was about to go up to where it was obviously meant to go and had to go, it drew back, said, in effect, "No, not yet," landed on that (to me) altogether surprising F-sharp. And it was that note, that pulling back, that always got me.

Then, in the chorus, the song went on up to where it had to go.

Jolly Boating Weather

39

But even then there were a couple of surprises. It would have been easy to end the song with the last four lines sung just once instead of twice. Once again the song draws back, says, "Not yet," before coming up to its thrilling close. And that last low C, on "ta-*ble*," instead of the expected G, is a final surprise. It must have been a wonderful song for the young men for whom it was written. It was certainly a wonderful song for us to sing, perhaps our favorite of all.

3

Swinging at Exeter

The Big Bands

I did not begin to listen seriously to music until I went away to school at Exeter, with about 750 other boys in grades nine through twelve. The music I heard there was the big band swing of the middle and late 1930s, wonderful music, full of melody, rhythm, and spirit, played with tremendous skill and exuberance by gifted musicians. I loved it then and do now.

I did not hear much of this music in my first year at school (1936–1937). We ninth graders, or "preps," were housed together in two prep dormitories, Dunbar and Webster. In these dorms, I'm not sure we were even allowed to have record players; at any rate, no one that I knew did. My first whiff of the music came in the fall of 1936. For the Fall Dance, the school had engaged Count Basie and his band, then at their very peak. He was to lead many fine bands in the next forty years, but perhaps none as great as this. The big dance was in the evening, in the basketball court of the gym, all prettied up for the occasion. From the metal girders over the middle of the dance floor hung a huge, slowly turning sphere, covered with little bits of glass that reflected all over the room the colored spotlights that shone on it. In the late afternoon, after all the athletic events were over, there was a short so-called tea dance. Most of the usual entrances to the basketball court were sealed off; the only way in, guarded by ticket takers, was through the big door to the outside. But from the top of one stairwell we could see through a window just a little of the dance floor and, on a raised platform at the side, the band itself. There was an impression of light and vivid color, of men with shiny instruments, and a bright and powerful sound. But that sound was meaningless to me; I had not yet learned to listen to it, to hear what was in it, even to know the sounds of the instruments that made it. It would be another four years or so before I would begin to know and love the music that Count Basie and his men were making that afternoon. Knowing what I know now, how I wish I could turn back a time clock and spend a few hours in that gym listening to him, and Buck Clayton, Sweets Edison, Dicky Wells, Jo Jones, Herschel Evans, Lester Young, and the rest.

In my second year at school I began to listen to swing records. My first real favorite, whose music (from that 1936–38 period, at least) I like to this day, was Tommy Dorsey. The jukeboxes all over town were playing his recording of "Song Of India," still famous. Like most of his instrumental recordings at that time, it was a swing arrangement of an old and famous tune. In these Dorsey would begin by playing the theme on his trombone against a soft, gently swung background. Nobody has ever done this better; he had a marvelous tone, and a way of phrasing that was so natural that you weren't conscious of it at all. After his solo came some music for the whole orchestra, then some solos, generally by Johnny Mince on clarinet, Bud Freeman on sax, Dave Tough on the drums, and, best of all, Bunny Berigan on trumpet. He was my first love on that

Swinging at Exeter

instrument, and though I have since heard many other players whose work also excites and moves me, he is still my favorite. He was apparently a very unhappy man and, when still young, drank himself to death. Something of this sadness is in all of his great solos. Beyond that, they were melodically extraordinarily inventive. Since Dorsey built most of his arrangements on classical or semiclassical themes, Berigan could not stay in the conventional jazz-blues pattern on which most solos were built, but had to improvise around different harmonic patterns. He was amazingly good at this; in all the jazz I've heard, I have never found anything better than his famous solos on "Song Of India" and "Marie." His solos were songs in themselves. Perhaps my favorite of all is the little-known solo he did on Dorsey's recording of "Liebestraum." Whatever hint of sadness may lie in that simple tune, he multiplied a hundred times in his solo—heartbreak in music. Yet it fits the song, so much so that I can't hear the song without hearing the solo. It was the first record I ever bought, and I still have it.

As I listened to these records and came to know them better, I began to whistle along with them, first the arrangements, then the solos as well. I had never whistled much before, but this music excited me so much that I wanted to take part in it, and be part of it, and whistling was the only way I could do it. Indeed, as I whistled I was in fantasy actually part of the band, now playing brass, now sax or clarinet. I also developed a kind of soundless whistle which I used when whistling out loud seemed the wrong thing to do. The soundless whistle had another advantage—by bringing my lips close together and forcing the air between lips and teeth I could make a sound that for me represented the brass section, while by using the back of my tongue and throat—rather like the "ch" in the German "ach"—I could make a sound to represent the reed section. Both sounds could be varied in pitch, and so equipped I could, so to speak, take my own swing band with me wherever I went. This is something I still like to do.

By my third year at school, like many of my schoolmates, I was a devoted, not to say fanatic listener. I had become friends with a boy who had a big collection of Benny Goodman records. He also had a custom-made record player that his father, an electrical engineer, had built for him. It was larger than the little boxes the rest of us used, and was housed in a black metal case painted with the crinkly black paint that seems to go with exotic machinery. It looked much better than anything we were used to, and it was; it was high fidelity for its time, and I listened to it as much as I could.

The school rule was that there could be no playing of record players after 8 P.M. There were radios in the common rooms, or "butt rooms," which we could play until 10 P.M., but we could not have radios in our rooms. I suppose the idea was that if we had radios, we would be tempted to break the eight o'clock rule in order to hear certain late programs, while with record players, which we could play anytime, we would be less tempted. We were tempted anyway. Every so often we would be overcome by the urge to hear a really fine record *after* 8 P.M. The teachers' rooms were close to our own; to play a record player out loud, even very softly, was too risky. But my friend (or perhaps his scientific father) had worked out a solution. He had figured out that sound can be conducted through the bones of the jaw, and had used this knowledge to make a great invention. He would push a steel needle through the eraser of a pencil. Next he would start the record playing, but with the volume turned all the way down, so that no sound came out of the speaker. Then one of us would hold one end of the pencil between his teeth, and put the needle, held by the eraser, on the grooves of the record. The needle picked up the sound from the record grooves, and the sound ran up the pencil, through teeth and jaws, and into our ears. It was not high fidelity, even by the standards of those days, but it worked; we

Swinging at Exeter

really could hear the music. Sometimes, late at night, two or three of us would be there, all bent over the spinning turntable, each with a pencil gripped between his teeth.

Many of the bands we hired for our dances were just getting started, full of excitement and enthusiasm, playing as well as they would ever play. I remember when Harry James was announced for one of the dances. We all knew him from his playing in Benny Goodman's band and wondered what his own band would be like. Suddenly the word was out that he had made a new recording of his theme song, "Ciribiribin." We rushed to hear it. The record began with a very schmaltzy, traditional rendering of the tune, in waltz time, no less. We stood around the record player, aghast. *This* was Harry James's band! *This* band was going to play at our Fall Dance! Just as we could stand no more the record broke into a swinging, up-tempo version of the tune, and we breathed a great sigh of relief. Once again we knew we were going to have good music. And indeed, of all the bands I heard at school, that early James band was one of the best.

Berigan's band was also very good. He was drinking heavily then. I remember, late in the evening, standing up close to the bandstand while he played "I Can't Get Started" and others of his great pieces. He was playing his trumpet with one hand, holding on to the mike with the other, and I suddenly realized with a thrill of excitement that he was holding onto the mike to keep from falling down. Even drunk he played beautifully.

At about that time something else happened in the world of recordings that caused great excitement among us jazz lovers. All records up to that time had been ten-inch 78 rpm records, with a playing time of about three minutes. But RCA Victor, who recorded Benny Goodman, Tommy Dorsey, and Bunny Berigan, one day put out perhaps three or four twelve-inch recordings. The most famous of these was, of course, Benny Goodman's "Sing, Sing, Sing." Instead of being three minutes long, it ran for twelve minutes; it seemed positively symphonic in scope. There was time for a much more extended arrangement, all in the kind of minor mode that we found exciting; for much longer solos, including a dramatic one by Harry James; and above all, for what seemed like hours of thrilling tom-tom drumming by Gene Krupa. We had never heard anything like it. I listened to it over and over again, learned all the solos, even learned to drum out on a table edge Gene Krupa's rhythmic riff. What excitement! Another one of those twelve-inch records featured Berigan's famous "I Can't Get Started" and, on the other side, a superb version of "The Prisoner's Song," with, at the very end, a few bars of Bunny playing the most mournful and heartbroken trumpet playing I have ever heard. He literally made his horn weep.

Jazz Whistling

Sometime during my third year at school I began a new part of my musical life. One day, as I was whistling one of the many swing records I had learned by heart, the thought came to me, "Why not make up some jazz solos of your own?" I decided to try it. I may have thought it would be easy. It turned out not to be. The first results were terrible. I could whistle only a few notes of the simplest, most banal kind of blues. But I kept at it, and the solos slowly became better. They tended (and still tend) to stay within the basic metrical and harmonic pattern of blues and swing that I was used to: eight bars of solo in a given key, eight more bars, a variation of the first but in the same key, an eight-bar bridge passage in a different key, and then eight closing bars in the original key. Most jazz arrangements and solos, and most of the popular songs of the times, were in this pattern. The harmonic pattern, too, was simple, though I still don't know enough musical theory to say what it was. But within those simple patterns the great musicians of the thirties did some wonderful things. Inspired by them, my own jazz whistling became freer, more melodic and inventive. Some of the time it was still rather labored and predictable, but every now and then I would surprise myself. I would hear in my mind, or whistle soundlessly or even out loud, a solo so varied, unexpected and just all-around *right* that it was as if I had not "thought of it" at all, but it had been made somewhere else and just happened to come out *through* me. This sometimes happened when I had been listening to a lot of good jazz and swing and had been inspired by it. But it quite often happened when I had not been whistling jazz for some time, or even hearing it or thinking about it. It was as if the sub- or unconscious creative music-making part of my mind had been busy for some time making something good, and was now ready to show it to me.

One winter evening around 1948, when I had not heard any jazz or swing, live or recorded, in some time, I was going with my sister and her husband to a little night spot in Poughkeepsie. As we went in, a jazz trio—piano, drums, and bass—were playing. Even though we could hardly hear them over the din of voices in the packed little room, I could tell they were good. Something in the lightness and crispness of their rhythm touched a musical button in me, and as we stood in the lobby taking off and checking coats, hats, boots, etc., and waiting for a table, I began to whistle a long solo that absolutely amazed me. To the critical mind inside me it seemed the best I had ever done, and a very good solo even by the standards of the music I listened to. Another voice inside was saying, "Holy Smoke! Where in the world is this coming from?" For two full choruses, sixty-four bars' worth, the music poured out of me. Then it was over, and I could not remember a note of it. But it was a fine moment.

Sometimes, then and now, the music maker inside would

deliver up to me not just solos, but complete jazz or swing arrangements, with solos included. Since the swing and jazz pieces of the times, except for "Sing, Sing, Sing" and a few others, were all about three minutes long, to fit on one side of a ten-inch 78 rpm record, most of my made-up arrangements fit this format—thirty-two bars of the jazz tune, two or three solos, and then a closing statement, a jazz coda. Once, though, influenced by "Sing, Sing, Sing" and the harmonic possibilities of the song, the inner music maker produced a long arrangement, with solos, of "Bei Mir Bist Du Schön" (which the song rhymed with "explain"). As I was doing and hearing this arrangement, it seemed very good. But once over, it was gone. Another time there was a more Basie-like arrangement, which I named "Palomar Stomp." (The Palomar was a ballroom in L.A. at which many big bands played. I had never been there, but liked the name.)

Did I ever think of learning to write music so that I could write down some of these tunes and arrangements? As far as I can recall, even in my world of fantasy no such thought ever crossed my mind. In those days I was a passenger in the car of life, not a driver. I accepted what came to me, and dealt with it as best I could. It had not yet occurred to me that I might actually decide what I most wanted to do, and take steps to do it. That part of my life would only begin some years later, and not with music.

Fantasia *and the Classics*

Not until my last year at school did I ever hear anyone play any classical records. A boy down the hall from me had a recording of Tchaikowsky's *Romeo and Juliet* which he played all the time. For some reason it annoyed me, I can't now think why. The big tunes, which were all I could hear over his tinny little record player, were fine swinging tunes, and would have made good raw material for a hot swing arrangement. Years later, when I met the piece again, I loved it, and still do. Maybe if I'd heard it at school on a really good record player, I would have liked it then.

But during those same years the doors to classical music opened to me, without my knowing it, when I went to see Walt Disney's *Fantasia*. I loved it, even Deems Taylor and the business about the sound track, which would not have fooled a child much younger than I. I liked all the music, probably in part because what I was hearing was so much closer to the sound of a real orchestra than anything I had ever heard before. I liked the dramatic, spooky pieces best, "The Sorcerer's Apprentice" and, even more, "Night on Bald Mountain." I liked many of the pictures, too, above all the moment in "Night on Bald Mountain" when the great Satanic figure on the mountaintop opened his batlike wings, and, in "The Sorcerer's Apprentice," when it seemed as if the flood would wash everything away. And Mickey Mouse as the apprentice seemed just about right.

But only one piece of music made a lasting impression on me—Stravinsky's *Rite of Spring*. I had never heard a note of it, never even heard *of* it. But Sir Thomas Beecham once said that great music is music that penetrates the ear and sticks in the mind, and that music certainly penetrated me, right to the bone. A few weeks later I could probably not have whistled two bars' worth of the music of any other piece in the picture, but great chunks of the melodies of *The Rite of Spring* stuck in my mind until I heard it again some years later, and have stayed with me ever since. I can sing along with it as easily as with any of my old Goodman or Dorsey records, and even without the record I know by heart the tunes of at least three quarters of it.

The images certainly helped. Stravinsky himself disliked it, but making the film an allegory of the life of the planet Earth itself made it (for me, at least) far more powerful than any images of tribal dances could have been. In one place, however, Stravinsky's image does fit better than Disney's. After the uproar at the end of the first half of the piece, there is a long quiet passage called "The Pagan Night." I hardly ever find myself outside on a quiet, starry, country summer night without hearing it in my mind. Apart from that I don't think of any images anymore when I hear the music, the music itself is enough. One small exception: In the last movement there is a short motive, six or seven notes, going down two successive half tones, often given by muted trombones, sometimes by other instruments. To me it has never sounded like anything but maniac laughter.

Even though I don't think of them when I hear the music, two of Disney's images stick with me. The section "The Pagan Night" begins with a group of slow, archlike phrases played in soft, dense chords by almost the whole orchestra, as if the Earth itself were breathing. Then there follow some lighter, but also slow-moving and gentle melodies. These go on for a while until they are interrupted by a two-note phrase, a rising major second played by muted horns, very sinister, almost like a voice saying, "Look out!" In the film Disney showed us large, slow-moving plant-eating dinosaurs, peacefully feeding, then, at the two-note horn phrase, looking up in faint alarm. More slow melodies, until they are finally interrupted, this time insistently, by the horns, now playing a rising minor seventh (it is this music that I use to remember the interval of the minor seventh). About six of these horn calls, and then the whole orchestra comes crashing in with a jagged downward phrase, almost like someone falling downstairs, following which both tympanists (now I see only the orchestra), a stick in each hand, begin to whack their tympani with all their strength, bam! bam! bam! Disney made this the entrance of Tyrannosaurus

Rex, always a popular favorite, and the beginning of a fight between him and Stegosaurus. In the next movement we hear a sad march tune on muted brass, first soft, then very loud. Disney made this powerful and mournful music the accompaniment to a tragedy, the extinction of the dinosaurs. After the death of Stegosaurus, he shows us a drought-stricken earth under a blazing sun, and the dinosaurs marching, looking vainly for water. Even though I knew that Disney was reading human thoughts into dinosaur minds, and that they could hardly have been aware of their coming extinction, it was a powerful image, still vivid after almost forty years. For I have not seen the film since, mostly because I am afraid that seeing it might spoil my memories of it.

At any rate, whether because of the images that went with it, or because of the strangeness, power, and beauty of the music itself, *The Rite of Spring* went into my mind and stayed there. Not long after, I heard a member of the family who knew a lot about music and went regularly to concerts of the New York Philharmonic, sounding off about what a scandal and disgrace *Fantasia* was, and how it cheapened the music. I thought then and still think that she was absolutely wrong.

Mr. Landers

My first experience of serious music making, and my first inkling of what it might be like to be a musician, and what great joys might be had from it, came when in my last year at Exeter I joined the Glee Club. Most of us didn't join because of any love of music. What we were after was one more activity to list under our senior picture in the school yearbook. Like most students, we assumed that anyone seeing our picture would judge our importance on campus by the number of entries under it. For people with entries like "Varsity Football

(3)" or "*The Exonian,* Editor," or "Spring Dance, Chairman," this was not a problem. But we lesser folk felt we needed something extra. Why not the Glee Club? It was a thoroughly respectable activity—much more so than, say, the Chess Club. It took several trips each year to girls' schools to sing with their Glee Clubs, and such trips away from our all-male campus were a welcome change. Many of us may have enjoyed the singing we sometimes did in compulsory morning assembly (called Chapel, though it was not very religious)—I know I did. (One song we sang often was "Upidee.") The musical director, Arthur A. Landers, who led this singing, seemed a pleasant enough man. Like all people with double first initials, he was generally known to the students as A^2 ("A squared"), and if he was not one of our faculty heroes, at least we had never heard anything said against him. We also sang hymns in Sunday church (also compulsory), and though like most of my friends I was not at all religious, I loved to sing some of the fine old songs. "Once to every man and nation, comes the moment to decide," was a special favorite. If most of us were not very good singers and had not done much singing, at least we had never found any reason to dislike it. So into the Glee Club we went.

Luckily there was plenty of room for us. The year before, the school had had a magnificent Glee Club, one of the finest anyone could remember. Most of them had graduated, leaving Arthur Landers with only a handful of experienced singers. He needed all the voices he could get. There may have been some sort of auditions or tryouts, but they were not demanding; anyone who could carry a tune got in. Then began a strange encounter, Arthur Landers and us. For a while both of us must have suffered from a kind of culture shock. In his long career he can hardly ever have seen such a raw bunch of recruits. We might be able to carry a tune, but that was about all we could do. We had never done any choral singing, knew nothing about music, and could not read a note. He may have toyed for a moment with the idea of teaching at least some of us to read music, at least a little, so that we might get some help from the written notes we held in our hands. But the task was too great, there wasn't enough time, there were concerts coming up to be prepared, and to get this gang ready to sing a full program in time for the first concert was going to be all he could manage.

On our part, we had to get used to the demands and discipline of music, and also to him. On the whole, the teachers we admired and liked most tended to be rather tweedy pipe-smoking types, many of them coaches of sports and still active athletes, who often competed against us in faculty-student matches. In other words, men much like our businessmen fathers and their businessmen friends, not particularly intellectual (at least, as far as we knew) and not artistic at all. Mr. Landers did not fit into this mold. He was like no one we had ever known, a being from another world. He was, in short, an artist and musician.

It didn't take him long to win us over. What did it, more than anything else, was that he was serious about music, loved it, gave himself over to it without reservations, and expected us to do the same. One of the first songs he had us sing was "Sir Eglamore." It was sung in unison, I think *a capella,* that is, without any accompaniment. The tune itself was not very beautiful or interesting. The whole point of the song was in the words; I can see now that it was a kind of study in the pronunciation of consonants. The song began:

> Sir Eglamore, that gallant knight
> Fa, la, lanky down dilly,
> He took up his sword and he went for to fight
> Fa, la, lanky down dilly.

Mr. Landers

53

I can see us now as he presented this song to us, with the news that we were going to *learn* it, and *sing* it, and in front of *other people*. We sat in front of him, in rows, on bleachers. We had not yet learned how to behave at rehearsals, so there was still much nudging, whispering, poking of feet. We were in that frame of mind where we hardly dared look at each other, lest it start us laughing. And now here was this song. Fa, la, lanky down dilly, indeed! Did he expect us to sing *that?* Yes, he did, and told us to. So we tried it. What came out must have been some sort of confused rumble. We did not know how to sing consonants quickly and clearly, even if we wanted to. With these words we did not want to; in embarrassment, in fear of being laughed at by each other, we slurred over them even more. Mr. Landers would have none of it. Do it again, like this—and he would bare his teeth and show the tip of his tongue, pronouncing with extra clearness those ridiculous sounds. Of course we all laughed, perhaps with more than a little mockery or contempt. He may well have heard this, but he didn't care. What was important was not his dignity as a faculty member, but the music, getting these words right. Again exaggerating, he would sing the words once more, then tell us to sing them. And slowly, perhaps without our even knowing it, there must have crept into our minds the thought, "Well, if he isn't afraid of making a damn fool of himself, maybe I don't have to be afraid of making a damn fool of myself." And just as slowly, again hardly aware we were doing so, we began to give ourselves over to the work, began trying to sing the music right, the way he wanted us to.

For behind our elaborately cool and even cynical facades, we were ready, like most young people, to be serious about something, and (without knowing it) were looking for things worth being serious about. Those few among us who were skillful athletes found it in sports; another few found it in this or that extracurricular activity. Almost none of us found it in our

Swinging at Exeter

studies. We worked for grades, to get B's and A's if we were that type, to escape D's and E's if we weren't. But we didn't care, and on the whole, we didn't feel that our teachers cared. If they did, they didn't convey it to us. In four years at that school and four more at college, I remember only three or four teachers, if that many, who made me feel that they were deeply interested in, *loved*, what they were teaching. Or preaching. To our compulsory Sunday church came many of the leading ministers and theologians of the Northeast. With only one exception, they tried to *sell* us Christianity, as they might have tried to sell us a vacuum cleaner. They were hearty, man-to-man, plain-talking, and reasonable, and it rarely took us more than a few minutes, walking back to our dorms after church, to pick and blow their arguments to pieces. The exception was a man whose name I wish I could remember. He preached at school three times, I think, while I was there. Each time he told us, in unashamedly poetic language, what Christianity meant in his life. He exposed his heart to us, and after the service my friends and I walked home silent, close to tears, almost afraid to look at each other. How badly we needed, and how rarely we found, people who would talk to us that way, who would take us seriously enough to give unsparingly of themselves. In his rather different way, this is what Mr. Landers did.

Once we began to give ourselves to the music and to take our work seriously, we found it enormously challenging and interesting, and (except for the handful with musical experience) altogether different from anything we had ever done. We began also to realize that Mr. Landers was an extremely good teacher. I was not to see for many years that in one sense music is a very special kind of athletics; had I seen the parallel then, I would have said he was a great coach. He had to teach us a new set of coordinations. One of the first things we worked on, not easy even for expert musicians, was entrances and cutoffs, how to start singing, or stop, all at once. He would pick out a note, give us a signal to begin, and there would be half a dozen audibly different entrances. A signal to stop; same story. We did it over and over again, and doing it, learned in a way we had never known, to *pay attention*. We had also to learn how and when to breathe, how to pronounce vowels as well as consonants, how to use our voices, how to sing softly, and, hardest of all for the tenors, how to sing high notes without straining. I can hear Mr. Landers now, telling us to get those eyebrows down. When we strained, up they went, and we couldn't get them down until we stopped straining. Later he conveyed this with a gesture, his two hands above his own eyebrows, moving them down. Still later, he could tell us with a look.

Once he had us divided up into first tenors, second tenors, baritones, and basses, he had to seat us in a way that would make best use of his small group of good singers. In any unskilled singing group people tend to be either leaders or leaners. The leaders know the music and can read their parts at least well enough to know, with a fair chance of being right, when they are supposed to start (or stop) singing. The leaners know the music much less well and can't read the parts at all, so they listen carefully to the leaders and copy them. In a good year Mr. Landers could surround each leaner with leaders, so that they could hardly go wrong. This year it was the other way round; he had to spread his leaders around like raisins in a cake, each one surrounded by a group of leaners. I was a leaner; the leader in my section was a fine singer named Tom Bridge. But my ear, trained by all the jazz and swing I had heard, was quite good, so after a while I knew my parts well and could sing them with some security.

Nothing daunted by our lack of skill, Mr. Landers chose for us a fairly difficult program, some of which I have forgotten. Our most important piece, which we sang (in English) with girls' glee clubs, was the second movement of the Brahms

German Requiem—"Behold All Flesh Is As the Grass." Even as we prepared it, without the two top parts and with only Mr. Landers accompanying on the piano, we knew it was noble and beautiful music. The first time we sang it with a girls' glee club, and heard all four parts, it was very exciting. It was even more exciting and moving, years later, when I heard the whole *Requiem* sung by an expert church choir in New York City, accompanied by a large organ, and more exciting yet when I first heard a recording of it, with the trombones in the introduction to the second movement leading up to those words I had loved to sing. Many years after that a friend of mine sang it with the Harvard-Radcliffe Glee Club and the Boston Symphony. I remember her telling me that going back to college after the concert, she and her friends, unable to stop singing, sang the movement "How Lovely Is Thy Dwelling Place" in the subway all the way back to Cambridge. How I envied her that experience.

It was our main vowel song. We learned from Mr. Landers that we could not sing long vowels in exactly the way we said them in speech. "Is" had to be sung more like "ease," "as" more like "oz," "grass" had to become "grah-h-hss." Later, when the music became jubilant and we were singing "Gladness! Gladness!" at the top of our voices, we had to make something halfway between "glad" and "glahd." Otherwise the results would be terrible, as Mr. Landers was always ready to show us, singing an exaggeratedly nasal "Is," "Grass," and "Gladness," which always made us laugh. But he got the point across. We learned, too, in singing a long sound like "grass," to delay the "s" sound until the last instant, instead of the "grassssssss" which we produced the first dozen or so times.

Our main song for men's voices alone was Randall Thompson's "Tarantella," set to the words of a poem by Hilaire Belloc. It was our most difficult piece, both in words and music. The music was not atonal, but the melodies and harmonies

Mr. Landers

were stranger and harsher than anything we were used to, hard to get into our ears, hard to sing in tune. My recollection is that the last part of the song, a slow dirge ending with the word "Doom," much stretched out, was sung without the piano. Then, after we cut off our last note, the piano matched that note with a final chord. If we had slipped off in pitch, that piano chord would show it. Even in rehearsal this was embarrassing. Out would come our last "Do-o-o-om," and then (like doom), the chord, a half tone or more higher. Though he might make a quizzical face, Mr. Landers said nothing; nothing needed to be said. As concert day came closer, and we became more nervous, I think we half hoped that if we slipped off pitch Mr. Landers would cover our error by playing a piano chord to match us. But we knew him well enough to know he would not. I now see that even if he had tried to cover up our error by cheating on the final chord—a musical Watergate— any skillful musician would easily have detected both error and cover-up. But he was not the kind of man to have done it, even if he could have gotten away with it.

I learned, among many other things, that one of the more helpless feelings in life is to be singing in a chorus which is gradually going flat. You hear it, you know it is happening, but you can't do a thing about it. You have to sing along with everyone else, even though you know it is not right. Perhaps a really strong and experienced singer could hold the proper pitch and so keep everyone else in tune, but there were none like that among us. As time went on, more and more of us were able to tell when we were going or had gone flat, but we could rarely keep it from happening.

In between the work we would relax now and then, and Mr. Landers would talk to us about things musical. One day he told us something interesting that years later I was to remember and put to use. Someone had mentioned tone-deafness, and he interrupted to say there was no such thing. We were astonished, having heard for years about "monotones" and people unable to carry a tune. He went on to say that about one out of some very large number of people, perhaps a hundred thousand or more, had no pitch discrimination whatever, quite literally could not tell high notes from low notes. Such people were easy to spot, because their speech was peculiarly toneless, without any of the usual inflections, the risings and fallings of ordinary speech. But apart from these almost freaky people, none of whom had we probably met, nobody was tone deaf. People who could not sing in tune could hear tunes as well as anyone else; they had simply not learned to coordinate voice with ear. He went on to describe how he had in fact taught some of these people to sing. The trick was to sound a note on the piano and ask the person to sing it, telling him to sing it higher or lower, until he finally matched it; then, after a few seconds of letting him experience the sensation of singing and hearing the same note, play a new note, and do the same thing. After a while, usually quite soon, the person was able to sing whatever note he heard, and the problem was solved. This went into the back of my memory file for many years, until one day, by this time a teacher myself, I used it to teach a "tone-deaf" student of mine to sing.

"Tarantella" was also full of vowel problems. The poem, and song, begin with the lines, sung quite fast:

> Do you remember an inn, Miranda
> Do you remember an inn.

This tended to come out "Dyourmbran inn." How we struggled with those lines. We had to learn to make an Italian "r," with the tip instead of the back of the tongue. Many showings of tongue and teeth from our director, who throughout all these trials remained insistent and strict, yet good-humored and patient. Bit by bit, we got it. Later we had to sing:

Mr. Landers

And the tedding and the spreading
And the straw for a bedding
And the bees
That tease
In the hi-i-igh
I-i-i-i-i-igh Pyrenees
And the wi, i-i, i-i-i-ine
That tasted of the tar.

It was one of the most exciting points of the song. We had to learn to land hard on those t's and d's and b's, almost to spit them out. Exaggerate them! he told us. In the same way, those divisions in the word "high" had to be sharply articulated; I still remember his excruciating slipping and sliding imitation of the way we were doing it.

Our big number, with which we closed all our joint concerts, was "Dance a Cachucha," from *The Gondoliers*, a rousing song, but with problems of its own—no fast Gilbert and Sullivan song is ever easy to sing. At one point we sang:

To the pretty
pitter, pitter, patter
And a clitter, clitter, clitter, clatter
Clitter, clitter clatter
Pitter, pitter, patter
Clitter, clitter, clatter, clitter, clitter

More work for the tongue and teeth.

So much for the music we sang—I wish I could remember all of it. Against all odds he made a chorus out of us. By the time of our first concert we were respectable, though neither powerful nor elegant, still a far cry from the Glee Club of the year before. Our concerts with the girls' glee clubs went well. One was particularly pleasant, the school relaxed and welcoming, the girls attractive and friendly, with a good concert to top it off. We continued to improve, and came up to our final concert of the year, a joint concert with the Beaver Country Day School (then for girls only), hopeful and confident that we would do well. We sensed, too, that this concert was particularly important for Mr. Landers. Since of all our concerts it was the one closest to Boston, it was the one to which a number of his friends went to see what he had been able to turn out this year. Did he tell us this? It seems unlikely, and unlike him. Did we hear it from veteran Glee Club members? Did we just assume it? I can't remember. Anyway, for whatever reason, when we climbed in our buses for the trip to Beaver, we felt that this was the big game.

The plan was, as usual, to rehearse with the girls, then have a short tea dance, then supper, then the concert. The rehearsal was a disaster. The girls began with some of their songs, and sang badly, worse than any glee club we had sung with. Perhaps this threw us off—when our time came we sang worse than we had since very early in the year. If we had been over-confident, soon we were nervous almost to the point of panic. Poor Mr. Landers must have been in despair. All those things he had struggled to teach us, and that we had learned, we now forgot. We missed entrances, forgot words, sang off pitch. The joint rehearsal, of the Brahms and the Gilbert and Sullivan, was the worst of all. We were sick about this; we had wanted to do well, for our sake and his. We went to the dance and dinner like people going to an execution. The girls did little to put us at our ease; perhaps they were as nervous as we were. My own dinner partner was by a factor of roughly ten even shyer than I was; I don't recall her saying a word throughout the meal.

Too soon it was concert time. In a spirit of "let's get this over with" we took our places on stage and sang our first two pieces. Perhaps because we were so sure we would do badly that we had stopped worrying about doing well, we were able to give ourselves to the music. Anyway, we made no mistakes. By the end of the second song, the thought was beginning to creep into our minds, almost against our will, "Well, nothing has gone wrong so far, maybe this won't be so bad." We began to breathe easier and to sing better. By the time we came to our Brahms *Requiem*, we had begun to hope that we might even do quite well. Early in the song the girls made some terrible mistake on an entrance. Most of the time it would surely have thrown us off. Perhaps because we were concentrating so hard, this time it did not. We hung in there, and Mr. Landers was able to get the girls back in step. His face showed pride and pleasure in our singing. By the end of the song our mood had changed. It was no longer even a question of getting by; we knew that by some miracle we were singing better than we had ever done. Like an athletic team on a winning streak, we were suddenly hot. Could we hold onto it? In that very different spirit of tension, full of hope rather than fear, we sang "Tarantella." We had never sung it as well; adrenaline kept us on pitch; the piano chord at the end was right on the button. Mr. Landers, reprieved as by a miracle, was beaming at us. I remember suddenly being aware that I was literally soaked in sweat, far more than I had ever been at any other concert. As we came into our final piece, the Gilbert and Sullivan songs, it was with the feeling of "We can't lose now, we've done it." In that spirit, a kind of ecstasy of pride, exhilaration, and happiness, we sang "Dance a Cachucha." The girls, perhaps rid of their own nervousness, perhaps carried along by us, were now singing strongly and well, and so we brought the concert to a fine close. There was applause, we left the stage, said good-bye to our dates, went to our buses, all half in a daze. As we gathered round the buses, Mr. Landers called us all together for an announcement. He told us that though he had had over the years many glee clubs with many better singers, he had never heard a glee club sing a more consistently musicianly concert. Musicianly! We were gladdened, and at the same time moved almost to tears by this compliment, which we knew was wholly sincere and well-deserved. In this exalted state, hardly speaking, we returned to school.

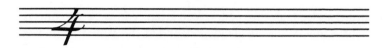

Stravinsky and
Woody Herman:
College and the War Years

Freshman Glee Club

I came to college eager to sing. Early in the fall there was an announcement about tryouts for the Freshman Glee Club. Candidates were to appear at such and such an office between such and such times. On the given day I showed up. Someone behind a desk handed me a form to fill out, then asked me to sing a scale. I sang a few notes, until he made a signal to stop, and showed that the tryout was over. "You will hear from us before long," he said. And so I did. A short time later I found in my mailbox a printed form card from the Freshman Glee Club. On it a box had been checked—Not Accepted. There was space for a few notes, on which someone had written, speaking (I supposed) of my voice, "Foggy, throaty, wheezy." So began and ended my music-making career at college.

I can see now that I was not very smart about this. I did not know yet that at the college, much more so than at school, the Glee Club was one of *the* things to do. But I should have figured out, anyway, that many people with singing experience would be trying out for the Glee Club, and that it would be as hard to get into as a major athletic team. I could at least have done a little singing, a little warming up, to get ready for the tryouts. But I didn't. I had hardly sung anything since our last concert the previous spring. It never occurred to me, fresh from that school experience, that someone wanting to sing as much as I did would be turned away. I went into the tryout confident, and absolutely cold. I suppose my voice was about what they said it was. Since they probably had many candidates to weed out, this was probably as efficient a way to do it as any.

Still, this rich college could and should have found a way to make it possible for people like myself who wanted to sing in a chorus, to do so. There was plenty of rehearsal space—I have since had many orchestra rehearsals in worse spaces than could have been found there for a second-team glee club. In the music school there must have been many student conductors who would have been glad to have the experience of conducting a choral group. The college, through its intramural sports program, made it possible for anyone who wanted to play a sport to do so. Why couldn't as much have been done for singers? Perhaps there were on campus other less important singing groups that I might have tried to get in. But I didn't know about them, and no one told me about them. Had I been then more the kind of person I am now, I might have tried to get together with some other glee club rejects to form a chorus of our own. But I had none of that kind of initiative or confidence. So—except for occasional more or less drunken singing of "I've Been Working on the Railroad" and similar songs— there was to be no music making for me at college.

People who know of my love for music today often say to me, "Don't you wish that your parents had made you take music lessons when you were little?" The answer is, No, I don't. I think that such forced exposure would probably have turned me away from music, as it has so many others. But it still makes me regretful, and angry, that when I had found out, almost by accident, that I loved making music and wanted more than anything to make some more, a rich university, dedicated (so they say) to the higher things of life, could have found nothing better to do than slam the door in my face.

Charlie Barnet for Dinner

Many of my college friends had big record collections. Through them I began to hear more early Benny Goodman, which I liked very much. In English class I read for the first time Hemingway's *A Farewell to Arms*. It made a great impression on me, especially the sad ending. At the same time I heard, many times, an old Benny Goodman record called "Madhouse," an up-tempo arrangement by Jimmy Mundy, beginning with a fine solo on muted trumpet by Bunny Berigan. In the middle of the recording there is a long piano solo by Jess Stacy. Why it should have struck me as sad I don't know; it is quick, rhythmic, and swinging. But it seemed to me the essence of melancholy. Somehow that piano solo and *A Farewell to Arms* got stuck together in my mind, and still are; one always makes me think of the other.

But the music I heard most and loved best during those years was the music of Charlie Barnet. I had never heard any of it before, had barely heard of him. This was partly because his band did not really begin to find its style and to make great music until 1939–40. At any rate, two or three of my close friends were real Barnet nuts, had almost all his records, and were always on the lookout for others. They had a very good record player, and we spent a lot of time together in their room listening to the music. Barnet had what was for me, with the exception of Ellington's, by far the most original and exciting band of that time.

Stravinsky and Woody Herman

One day Barnet's band came to the city to play a two- or three-day date in a big movie theatre. Like pilgrims to Mecca, we rushed to hear him—none of us had ever heard him in person. The stage show only gave him time for eight numbers or so, including some of our favorites. Wild with excitement, our courage fanned to a hot flame by the music, we cooked up what was for us, all timid outsiders, a daring scheme—we would go backstage, say hello to Charlie Barnet, and ask him to have supper with us in the college dining room. Egging each other on, scared but determined, we found him backstage, thanked him for the fine music, and made our proposal. He was very nice, but as we feared, said, "Thanks a lot fellas, but we've got another show coming before long, and I'd love to do it but I just can't make it. . . ." In the middle of this he suddenly looked at his manager and said, "What the hell, how much time have we got?" The manager said something about an hour, an hour and a half. He said to us, "You guys far away?" We said no, only a few blocks, hardly daring to believe what we were hearing. He said, "Let's do it," and he, the manager, and I and my three friends climbed into a couple of cabs and went off to the dining hall. Into the dining room we went, got a table, ate the usual crummy food, while Charlie Barnet, perfectly at his ease and enjoying the little comedy, filled our ears with tales of the music business and of his own colorful life. I remember him describing some Mickey Mouse band as "Boris Seeley and his Seldom Fed Seven." There was some turning of heads, but even the biggest bandleaders were not the kind of cult heroes that rock stars would later be, and many people did not know who our guest was. Those who did must have been wondering (so we felt) how these three unknown sophomores had pulled off such a coup. The time flew by, too fast, and after a while Charlie Barnet thanked us and said he had to get back. We thanked him, walked out to the street with him, and said more thanks and good-byes as he and the manager got into a cab and drove off. Back we went to the college, and to questions—"Was that . . .?" "How did you . . . ?" "Where did you . . . ?" It was one of the (few) high points of my college years.

The Return of The Rite

About a year later I was living in another entry in the dorm, on the third floor. Every evening after dinner it took me about three hours to get up those three flights to my room, because on the first and second floor there were several groups of guys that I always liked to stop and talk with. In one room on the ground floor lived a quiet pair whom I knew only slightly. They had an extremely good record player, a Capehart, the super hi-fi of those days, and played nothing but classical music, which interested me no more than it ever had. But one day in their room, looking idly at the spines of all the record albums in their cabinet, I suddenly saw *The Rite of Spring*. Memories of *Fantasia* and of Stravinsky's music, which I had not thought about in a long time, rushed in on me. I thought to myself, "I wonder how I would feel about that music if I heard it without the pictures." So I told my friend about the film, and how that music had gripped me, and asked if someday when he was out or not busy I might come and play his album and see whether I still liked it. He said okay, showed me how to work the machine, and we set a day and a time. Came the day, I went to his room, and with great curiosity and excitement took out the album, put on the first record, and waited for the music to begin. A second or two and there it was, the high bassoon solo playing that strange wandering tune. I knew it! To my surprise and delight, it was as familiar as if I had heard it the day before. The music had lost none of its power over me. As I put on record after record—these were 78 rpm's—I half feared that the spell would break, that there would be parts of the music that I would not like or that would bore me. But no; from the first note to the last the music kept its grip on me. At one and the same time I felt the delight of recognition and the equal delight of discovery, like seeing an old and dear friend after a long absence. Time flew by, stopped, didn't exist. Too soon the music ended. But by then, *I knew.* I loved this music, had to have it. Soon after, I bought an album of my own, and played it often, at college and at home, on my own little record player. My mother used to say that every time I put it on our cat ran out of the house. A hint? If so, I ignored it. But perhaps not; my mother didn't like my swing music much, and this was a welcome change.

Later, before I went into the Navy in 1943, I bought the album of *Shéhérazade.* Where did I hear it? Did my classical-music-loving friend invite me to listen to some others of his albums, and wisely suggest this one? Did I hear it on the radio? I can't remember. I also bought Stravinsky's *Firebird*—the suite, not the complete ballet. These were the beginnings of my classical collection, and of my love for classical music.

An Evening with Woody Herman

When the war ended the Navy sent our submarine, the *Barbero,* back to the Mare Island Navy Yard, north of San Francisco, to be decommissioned, or as the saying went "put in mothballs." It was a frustrating time. Directive followed directive; what we did one week, we often had to undo the next. Our wartime sense of purpose was lost. All we really cared about was getting enough points to get out of the Navy and resume our normal lives, whatever they might be. But, at least for those of us who loved jazz music, there was one bright spot. Through radio programs and records we began to hear the music of the 1945–1946 Woody Herman band, or Herd as it was called. It was tremendous music. Herman was a good though not a great jazz player, but he had then and has had ever since the ability to gather round him, hold together, and inspire very talented and imaginative musicians. The band he put together in 1945 was, for me at least, by far the most exciting big band of the time, and the equal of any band of any time. Nothing they did was routine; even the most ordinary ballads (as people then called popular songs), they played with great imagination, wit, and spirit. Their swinging numbers were in the jazz-swing tradition, and yet in many ways different, full of surprises. They had a number of brilliant and inventive soloists, one of whom, Bill Harris, played the trombone in a way that no one had ever played it before. Above all, they played with a sense of commitment and enthusiasm that was simply hair-raising.

They had been playing on the East Coast, and one of the many reasons I was eager to get out of the Navy was so that I could go hear them. Just as I was getting close to the date of my discharge, I heard terrible news—the Herman band was going to come to the West Coast to play for a couple of months, and was then going to break up. I was going to miss them! I would never hear them! I was such a timid and conventional young man that it never occurred to me, not for a second, that I might stay out on the West Coast, arrange to get discharged there, see something of California and the Northwest, and hear Woody Herman in the process. But no, my home was in the East, and when the war ended I had to go home. So it was with a sense of great relief and excitement that I heard that they would be playing at a famous jazz spot, the Panther Room of the Hotel Sherman in Chicago, at the very time I would be going East. If I left as soon as I got my discharge, I could just catch them. With the usual last-minute rush, and a week of almost sleepless nights, we got the ship ready for decommissioning. The ceremony over, the flag pulled down, we walked for the last time off the ship on which we had spent a couple of years, and, eager as we were to leave the Navy, we felt a pang of loss and regret that surprised us. Then more frantic packing and rushing, and I was on my way to Chicago.

The following afternoon I presented myself at the Panther Room at about five o'clock. Since I was planning to stay until they closed up at two in the morning, and since I wasn't planning to drink, I thought I had better have dinner there, or I would get dirty looks from waiters and captains all night long, maybe even be thrown out. I went in, and there was Woody and the band, just starting to play. In those days before hi-fi, radios and record players were much further from the sound of the real thing than they are now, and it was always a glorious and stunning surprise to hear the sound of real live musicians playing their instruments. All the more so in this case. The Panther Room was not a very large room, and anyway, whenever the band began to play, I and quite a few other people went up and stood right in front of the bandstand until they finished their set. The Herd, in spite of a year and a half of long nights and constant travel, had lost none of their enthusiasm. On every number they put out a hundred per cent. The sound of those saxes, trombones, trumpets, blown with every last bit of strength of the players, and the sense of the physical effort it took to make those sounds, the flying fingers, strained necks, bulging cheeks—all this had a gut-hitting impact beyond the power of words to describe. I understand the attraction that loud music has for young people, and why they like to turn their amplifiers up as loud as they will go. But the loudest amplifier in the world can never make up for the excitement of knowing that human muscle, breath, energy is making the sounds I am hearing.

As was the custom, the band played fifteen- or twenty-minute sets, five pieces or so, followed by intermissions perhaps

An Evening with Woody Herman

71

a bit longer. One by one my favorite numbers appeared, along with many others I did not know. In between sets I went back to my table, ordered dinner, ate it, looked around at the other people, relished the music I had just heard, thought about the music I was soon going to hear, made fantasies about playing trumpet in the Herman band, and in general almost burst with joy and pleasure. I was more timid than now about telling people—writers, musicians, or whatever—that I liked what they had done. But after one set, ending with a real flag-waver called "They Went That Way," I couldn't hold back any longer. As the trumpet section came down off the bandstand I said to them, "That music you're making is terrific!" One of them looked at me, smiled a kind of dazed smile, as if he too was having trouble coming back down to earth, and said, "Yeah, it really is, isn't it?" As my sister Jane likes to say of people so happy that they can't contain it, they just couldn't wipe the smiles off their faces.

From five in the afternoon to two the following morning is nine hours. No nine hours ever went by faster. In spite of the many previous weeks of little or no sleep, I was not a bit tired. Every new set by the band charged up my batteries again. It seemed no time at all before Woody announced that this set would be the last. The band played, we all clapped and cheered, hoping against hope for more. But Woody said good-night, they packed up their instruments, and left. I paid my bill, left the Panther Room and the hotel, hardly knowing, as the old saying goes, whether I was on foot or on horseback. Next day I flew back to the East Coast, home, and my new life.

Stravinsky and Woody Herman
———— ————

5

I Meet Beethoven

Listening

In the fall of 1946, after I left the Navy, I began to work full time
at the New York City office of World Federalists, U.S.A., an
organization promoting world government. That seemed to me
the only way, in the long run, to bring about an end to war,
which the atom bomb had now made suicidal. Later in the fall I
moved into a residential club for single young men on East
Sixteenth Street. The other members of the house were varied
and congenial, and I enjoyed my two years there, that being the
limit anyone could stay. One of the members was a good jazz
pianist, another played the flute, and another played, among
other things, the Bach Toccata and Fugue in D minor (or much
of it) on the accordion, which the pianist nicknamed the Stomach Steinway. But that was about all the music we had. No one
in the house had a good record player or played classical records
on the house machine, which we used mainly at parties. Nor did
anyone in the house, as far as I knew, ever go to any kind of
classical concerts. Music was a very small part of our life.

It was at the house of my younger sister Sue that I began, around 1948, to listen seriously to some of the music of Beethoven, Brahms, and Mendelssohn. She had just married and was living in the country about an hour and a half north of New York City. On many weekends I used to go up to visit her and her husband, in-laws, and friends. I liked New York City, which I thought of as my home town, but the country was a pleasant change. In the summer we played tennis, swam, had picnics; in the winter, we skated; in all seasons we took walks. At night there were dinners, parties, dances. In between there were many quiet hours, and I spent many of these sitting in front of her record player, listening to some of her long-playing records. She had only a few—the Beethoven Violin Concerto, *Emperor* Concerto, and Seventh Symphony, the Mendelssohn Violin Concerto, the Brahms Violin Concerto, and perhaps one or two others. I listened to them over and over again, slowly learning more and more of them by heart, as I had learned many jazz records. Just as *The Rite of Spring* had opened for me the door to symphonic music in general, so these few records began to open the door to the great music of the eighteenth and nineteenth centuries.

The first and most important of these was the Beethoven Violin Concerto, played by Joseph Szigeti and the New York Philharmonic under Bruno Walter. I have often wondered why this should have been the first music of Beethoven's, and the first classical music, to catch my ear, rather than one of the symphonies or piano concerti. The sound of the violin, like that of the operatic soprano, takes getting used to. Like many people, when I first heard it I did not like it at all. Enemies of the violin then called it a "squeak box," which seemed to me close to the truth. Moreover, compared to many great violinists, Szigeti did not have a very beautiful tone—at least, not on this recording. I was not caught by the beauty of the *sound* of the instrument.

I Meet Beethoven

What I now think must have drawn me to that particular music is that in some important respects it was very like the jazz-swing music I already knew and loved. That is, the relationship between the classical orchestra and soloist was much like what it was in jazz. The orchestra stated the themes, and the soloist improvised on and around them, commented on them. This relationship is particularly strong in the Beethoven concerto; even in rapid passages the solo part is clearly related to one or another of the main themes. Also, in his performance of the concerto Szigeti always made those relationships clear. He was for me, and I mean this as the highest compliment, the Bunny Berigan of the violin. It helped me, too, that the themes themselves were strong, simple, clear, beautiful tunes, that (as Beecham said) penetrated my ear and stuck in my mind. Jazz musicians of the times might have called them good riffs. So I was very soon able to do what I had always done with my jazz records—imagine myself *making* the music I was listening to. I even began to learn the solo part, perhaps not every note, but well enough so that I could at least follow the soloist as I had once followed my neighbor in the school glee club.

The other thing that made this music grip me was that in the middle of the first movement (at measure 330, as I have just found by checking the score) Beethoven gives the soloist a lovely, plaintive melody in a minor key, not related, certainly not closely related, to any of the main themes of the movement. The very first time I heard this tune it surprised and moved me, as it did for many years afterward. This meant that the next time I heard the piece, I was waiting for that tune, listening for it. At two other places in the first movement the music made a particularly strong impact on me. At measure 216, and again at measure 490, the soloist enters into a number of measures of rapid passage work, seven the first time, six the second, while behind him some of the orchestra, the first time clarinets and bassoons, the second time oboes and horns (I never noticed the difference until just now, when I looked it up) play a long sustained note which slowly turns into a crescendo which in turn finally brings in the whole orchestra with a powerful statement of the second main theme of the movement. Tension, feeling more and more sure that something is going to happen, but not knowing exactly what or when, is one of the great sources of emotion in music, and Beethoven was a master of tension. The first time I heard that long note and crescendo, I was well into it before I knew it was happening. But after hearing it once or twice I began to listen for it, wanted to catch it as soon as it started, so as not to lose any of the excitement in it. Then, of course, I began to anticipate it, to hear when it was coming, so that from further and further away I could think, "Here it comes, we're getting closer and closer to it, we're almost there, *now!*"

Listening to a piece of music that we don't know but are beginning to know and love is much like going as a child to some much loved place where wonderful things happen, perhaps the house of a best friend or a favorite grandparent. At first the child only knows he is there when he gets there. But gradually he begins to learn more and more of the landscape on the way to the house, so that he can tell, at first, when he is within a block of it, and then later within two blocks, three blocks. The landscape all around the house, and for greater and greater distances, begins to take on some of the magical qualities of the house itself. This ordinary signpost becomes the special sign that says the house is eight blocks away, this tree, this fire plug, this traffic light, this bump in the road—all become magic signs, saying to the child, "You're getting closer, you're getting closer!" In time this magical quality can spread for hundreds of miles. When I was growing up I had such happy summers with Granny in Maine that the whole state became a magic place for me. Though Granny is long since dead and the house we loved burnt to the ground without a trace, and though I rarely if ever see most of the friends of those days, I cannot even now drive across the Maine state line without feeling that some unexpected and wonderful things may happen.

In the same way, when we hear in a piece of music a passage, even very short, that catches our ear, the special quality of that passage begins to spread out into the rest of the music. We begin listening for it, and the musical signs that tell us it is coming, earlier and earlier, and so begin to hear the other parts of the music in a different way. Of course, this doesn't work if we don't like the rest of the music, or if there are no *hearable* relationships between the bit we like and the rest, or if all stretches of the musical landscape are so alike, as is often the case with me with many modern pieces, that we can't tell when the part we like is coming or how close we are to it. But in a well-constructed piece of music, it only takes a few bars, a few notes, of special beauty, to draw us into the whole piece. There were many such special places, a few of which I have mentioned, in *The Rite of Spring.* In *Petrouchka,* one such place is a crescendo for brass that comes (twice) early in the piece. Another is the place—two places, to be exact—where after some solo work by the piano, the muted brass come in with Petrouchka's theme. It always makes my skin prickle. One of my favorite modern works for orchestra is a piece by Henri Dutilleux called *Métaboles,* which George Szell and the Cleveland Orchestra premiered here in Boston, and which Charles Munch recorded in France (a recording still available from the Musical Heritage Society). It is a very modern piece, written with all the latest serial techniques, but unlike most of that music, it is for me (like everything else by Dutilleux) intensely musical. The very first notes of the piece are strong, dissonant chords. But something about those dissonances, and the colors and sounds of the instruments making them, riveted my attention from the first note. I thought, "Wow!" I began to want to hear those same chords again, to hope that they were coming back, to listen for signs that they might be coming back. And indeed, at the end of the piece, they *do* come back. Meanwhile, everything in the piece is closely enough related to them so that they remain always in mind, and that sense of expectation, hope, excitement, is never lost. The composer is, so to speak, always saying (to me at least), "You like those chords, eh? You want to hear them again, do you? Well, just wait and listen. Maybe you'll hear them again, maybe you won't." Then, when the signs of their return become clearer and clearer, and they finally do return, it is like the return of that long crescendo in the Beethoven concerto, or the equally magical movement in the first movement of the Mendelssohn Violin Concerto when at the end of the soloist's cadenza the flutes and oboes tactfully interrupt his showing off by bringing back the opening theme of the movement, as if to say, "We're sorry to interrupt you, but we have to get on with this piece."

In this way the Beethoven Violin Concerto captured me. At the same time, it prepared me to hear and be captured by other music. It stretched out my time scale, enabled me to hear and remember as *tunes* much longer and more extended melodies than I had ever heard in my three-minute jazz records. Thus it enlarged, even as Stravinsky had in *The Rite of Spring*—and isn't this after all the proper business of all composers—my ideas of what a tune could be. So, when I began to listen to Beethoven's Seventh Symphony, I was not bored, as I might well have been only a little earlier, by the extended introduction. I had learned that something was going to happen, and to wait, to find out what it would be. And soon along came another one of those magical, mind- and heart-seizing moments of music. The main theme of the first movement comes in for the first time very softly, almost timidly, with the solo flute, slowly joined by some of the other instruments. Then, after a tiny pause, back it comes, this time with the whole

I Meet Beethoven

orchestra, in a blaze of exaltation. At the very end of the first movement is another such moment, when, after a long build-up by the master of tension, the horns sing out in triumph once again to end the movement. In the second movement, the first such moment for me came not in the main theme, beautiful as it is, but when the woodwinds, stating a kind of second or counter-theme, rose to a point and then descended in a series of extraordinarily rich and beautiful chords. The third movement, the Scherzo, I have always liked, but nothing in it grabbed my attention very much, except perhaps in the trio, the long sustained notes of the trumpets falling off at the end. But the last movement! From the first time I heard it, it carried me away. There are more moments of excitement in it than I can name, above all the long buildup to the final coda, for me still the finest *ending* of any of Beethoven's symphonies.

The Seventh Symphony soon joined *The Rite of Spring* as perhaps my favorite piece of classical music, and was for a long time my favorite Beethoven symphony. By now there is so much music that I love that I can no longer think of favorites. If I couldn't take at least fifty records with me to the proverbial desert island, I wouldn't go. I cannot even pick favorites among Beethoven's symphonies. They are different, and meet different needs in me. At some times nothing pleases me more than the lightness and wit of the First, or the Eighth; at other times, I like the gentleness and reflectiveness of the Fourth or Sixth; at other times, I want the weight of the Third, or Ninth. But the Seventh was the one that opened the door.

From the Beethoven violin concerto I went on to the Mendelssohn and then the Brahms, and soon came to love both. For many years, exploring music, I made a point of hearing every violin concerto I could find. These were my introduction to the music of Mozart, Tchaikowsky, Prokofiev, and Frank Martin, among others. For many years I gently reproached Beethoven for having written five concerti for piano and only one for violin, or Mozart for having written twenty-seven for piano and only five (all early) for violin. What troubles me more now is not that there are too few violin concerti, but that so many beautiful ones are so seldom played, such as (among others) those by Szymanowski (2), Bloch, Britten, Barber, Frank Martin, Larsson, Menotti, Nielsen, or Walton. At any rate, they were for me one of the great doors into music.

Barbershop Quartet

When I was living in the big house on Sixteenth Street we, like all young people, gave many big parties. At these we drank a lot, usually too much, and once drunk enough to overcome our shyness, did a lot of loud, boisterous, joyous singing. Just as at college, I loved this as much as anyone. To be in a group of people all singing the same song at the top of their lungs is, at least for the moment, to feel very much an insider, which was very important for me, who in those days usually felt more like an outsider. Also, it is a way of overcoming or losing one's shyness, fear of doing the wrong thing, worry about what other people are thinking. Finally, for me, it was a chance for the hidden ham actor to come out and take the stage. Singing songs like "I've Been Working on the Railroad," I used to like to "sing tenor," which meant singing above the melody in a very simple harmony, as loud as I could. Great fun.

One day one of my other friends in the house, the flute player, a good singer and musician, thought it might be fun to get up a barbershop quartet, and sing at parties, or perhaps at one of the church suppers across the street. Probably because of my party singing, he asked me if I'd like to be in it. I said I would. Since it was his idea, and since he had a fine voice, he would sing first tenor, that is, the melody. I would sing second tenor. After much cajoling we roped in a baritone and bass. We started with a repertory of three songs: "Graceful and Easy," "Mavourneen, Mavourneen," and "Aura Lee." As I could not read music, the leader had to teach me my parts, which I memorized. Singing in the quartet was much harder than the "singing tenor" I had been doing at parties. The harmonies were more complicated, and my part didn't sound very melodic all by itself. But after quite a few rehearsals we finally felt ready. The church people said they would love to have us sing at their church supper, and the date was set.

Came the day, and I found myself as nervous as I had ever been before a Glee Club concert. Here I had no one to lean on, I was all by myself, and if I made a mistake or forgot my part, everyone would hear it. When the time came, I stood up, sweating and trembling—probably only the poor baritone was more scared. But we did okay; once we got past the first few notes, the music took hold of us, the ham actor in all of us came out of his hiding place, and we threw ourselves into those fine songs. Much applause; a bow or two (but no encore, as we had sung all the songs we knew); and then, a bit exhilarated and a bit embarrassed, we sat down and slowly resumed normal life. We planned more singing, but soon after that the first tenor left the house to get married, and no one else knew or cared enough to keep the quartet going. But it was fine music, and I am sorry to hear, as I do now and then, that barbershop quartet singing is dying out.

The Brahms Requiem *Again*

About three or four years after I moved to New York, I began to go out quite a lot with a very nice young woman who also worked in the world government movement. One day I read that the choir of St. George's Church, right across the street from where I had lived, was going to sing the Brahms

German Requiem, with professional soloists, and accompanied by the big church organ. I asked my friend if she would like to go, she said yes, so we went. The first movement was a complete surprise to me. When we sang "Behold, All Flesh Is As the Grass" at school I had thought we were singing the whole Brahms *Requiem,* not just a part of it. But I was glad to know that there was more. As the organ began to play the introduction to the second movement, I realized how much grander and more tragic this music was than Mr. Landers had been able to convey on the piano. (How he would have loved to have an orchestra!) After the first phrases of the introduction, and just before the male chorus begins to sing for the first time, there is a sort of bridge passage, a series of very poignant four-note phrases. They touched something inside me; not only were my eyes full of tears but I soon had to struggle to hold back real sobs. The chorus sang its first statement of the theme, and I had barely gained control of myself before there was another, longer, grander, more somber introduction, followed by the return of the chorus, now *fortissimo,* surely one of the great moments in all music. More struggles with sobs; I shook all over. This was to happen several more times during that movement. From then on I was more or less safe; I loved all the requiem, but the later movements never quite gripped me as that second movement had.

As we were leaving, I told my friend about my struggles to keep from crying during the second movement. She said, yes, she had noticed. I said, "Well, just out of curiosity, what would you have done if I had come out with a few loud boo-hoos?" She said, very sweetly, "I would have tried to pretend it was me."

I Meet Beethoven

The Rite *in Concert*

I lived in New York City from the fall of 1946 to October, 1952, when I left to go to Europe. During those years I went to hardly any concerts, no more than two or three. As part of my work with the World Federalists I spent a great deal of time visiting our local chapters all over New York State, speaking to meetings of members or to other groups in the community. I had few evenings free, and when I did, was glad just to take it easy at home, read, and rest. Also, I had very little money, and though concerts were cheaper then than now, they were not cheap for me. My most important reason for not going to concerts, however, was a very foolish but typical one—it was just not part of my routine. I never even thought of doing it.

But near the end of my stay in New York there was one splendid exception. Listening to records, I had come to know and love not just the Seventh Symphony of Beethoven but also the Sixth, the *Pastoral.* I found the second movement very beautiful, and the long buildup to the climax in the last movement as exciting, in its different way, as the last movement of the Seventh. So when I read in the papers that in a New York Philharmonic concert Pierre Monteux would conduct both the *Pastoral* Symphony *and The Rite of Spring,* I decided that this was a double-header not to be missed. Feeling nervous, as we tend to when we do even a simple thing for the first time, I went to the box office and timidly asked if I could buy a ticket. Luckily they had one, in the balcony. On concert night there I was, as expectant and excited as when I had heard Woody Herman. I had been to a few concerts before, but I had always listened like a little child, bewildered even if fascinated by all the strange sounds I was hearing. Tonight would be different. To some degree I knew what I would be hearing. I could listen intelligently, could listen *for* things. Soon the orchestra took their places, tuned, Papa Monteux came out, and they began.

As with Woody Herman, I was dazzled by the difference between the sounds I had heard on records and the sounds now coming from that stage. The familiar and much-loved *Pastoral* became all the more lovely and moving; the great finale shook me to my bones.

Then, after intermission, *The Rite.* Before they even began to play, I was excited just by the number of musicians I saw crowding onto the stage. With all those people something exciting was bound to happen. The lights dimmed, the audience and orchestra quieted, Monteux came on again, a few seconds of silence, and then once again those high wailing notes from the bassoon, and I was off once more on a journey through that musical landscape I had come to know almost as well as the simplest song. But what a difference! If the recordings I had heard had failed to do justice to the sounds of the *Pastoral* Symphony, by a far wider margin they failed to do justice to *The Rite.* By now I am used to the glorious uproar of a great symphony orchestra in full cry. It excites me as much as ever, but I am not surprised by it. Hearing it for the first time, I was ready to jump right over the edge of the balcony.

Almost twenty years later, when I was an experienced concertgoer, I was in Los Angeles doing some lectures, and having always wanted to hear the Los Angeles Philharmonic in their own hall, I bought a ticket and went. Rafael Frubeck de Burgos was guest conducting an arrangement of his own of music by Albeniz, Mahler's *Kindertotenlieder,* and Berlioz's *Symphonie fantastique.* My seat was in the fourth row of the orchestra, two or three seats from the right-hand edge. Sitting in the four seats to my left were a family. Mother, Father, Teenaged Son, and Son's Teenaged Friend. They were right out of some comedy skit. The mother was clearly the music lover. The father, who somehow gave me the impression that he was a military officer out of uniform, had been dragged along against his will. However, he had prepared himself with quite a few cocktails, and by the time he arrived at the hall was half-seas over. He lolled back in his seat, went to sleep quite often, every so often woke up with a start and began boozily conducting the orchestra, and now and then leaned over to mutter something to me that I could not make out. The mother sat next to him, stiff with anxiety and irritation. Beyond her were the two boys, who also seemed to be there against their will. At intermission time their faces were as carefully bland and impassive as when they came in. After intermission, the *Symphonie fantastique,* a piece which for many years I actively disliked, and then suddenly came to love. The performance was glorious, the sound warm, vivid, and detailed—that hall has not been enough praised. Finally the last wild movement, the four *ta*-ta-ta-*ta*-ta-ta-*taaah's* from the trombones, and the great closing blaze of the whole brass section. While we were cheering and applauding, the family got up to go. As the two boys crossed in front of me, I said to the first one, in a voice as casual and noncommittal as I could make it, "How did that grab you?" He slowly turned a dazed look on me, and in an awestruck voice not much louder than a whisper said, "What a sound!"

Yes, indeed! What a sound! Music is not, as it has become the foolish fashion of the avant-garde to say, "Nothing but sounds and silences." It is much more than that. But surely it is, among many other things, the most glorious collection of sounds that people have ever invented. Children or adults who meet classical music for the first time should at least some of the time be able to meet it this way, as a great feast of sound, to be enjoyed for its own sake, without having to worry much about when or how it was made or what it is called or what it means. Let astonishment and delight come first; curiosity, questions, thought and understanding, will come later.

In this way, as I sat years before in Carnegie Hall, the sounds of *The Rite,* familiar as tunes but completely unfamiliar in their variety, intensity, brilliance, and power, were pouring

The Rite *in Concert*

over and through me. And as I listened I watched, fascinated by the furious but disciplined activity on the stage. I particularly remember one moment. In talking about *Fantasia*, I described a place where soft music from strings and winds is interrupted every now and then by two-note calls from the horns, sounding a note of menace. Finally the orchestra comes crashing in with what Disney, on the screen, made the entrance music for Tyrannosaurus Rex, and the beginning of a great fight between him and Stegosaurus. What I saw on stage, however, was even more exciting. There were two sets of tympani (kettledrums). A tympanist stood ready at each one, a stick in each hand. As the "fight music" began, both of them, using both hands, began to hit their drums, *as hard as they could!* It seemed to me then that they were actually raising their sticks above their heads, so great was the impression they gave of violence and power. Any dinosaur images I might have had in mind retired to a quiet corner of memory. Nothing could be as exciting as the sight of those musicians hitting those drums, in perfect unison, with all their might.

Soon the concert and the wild applause were over and I was on my way home, in much the same dazed and exalted state as I had been after hearing Woody Herman. I did not yet know it, but in my journey of exploration into music I had crossed another great divide. From now on, as I had listened to jazz music for many years, I would listen to classical music vicariously, that is, as if I were actually making it. In my imagination I would be, not in the audience, but on the conductor's podium, and, often at the same time, among the players. My fantasy life, always active, now began to include the possibility of being a classical musician. This was and is very important. Action *begins* with fantasy. We are very unlikely to do something new, difficult, and demanding until after we have spent some time imagining or dreaming ourselves doing it.

I Meet Beethoven

I Buy a Guitar

Around Christmas, 1951, I bought myself a guitar. I don't really remember why. I didn't know anyone who played the guitar. I was not a great lover of folk music, had hardly even heard any. Once or twice I had heard Vicente Gomez play some classical, some flamenco, and had enjoyed it, but not so much that it made me think, "I want to play like that."

Other things may have pushed me to it. The young woman who had gone with me to hear the Brahms *German Requiem* had found someone she liked better than me. That was a blow. More important still, I was beginning to be very dissatisfied with my work. At the same time, Senator Joseph McCarthy was becoming popular, and I began to see with surprise and dismay that most of my fellow countrymen did not know what civil liberties were all about, and did not care. All of this made me very unhappy. For the first and only time in my life I was having trouble sleeping. Night after night I would wake up at two or three in the morning, lie in bed for hours, unable to go back to sleep, until about an hour before getting-up time, when I would fall asleep as if drugged, sleep though the alarm, wake up late. Also, since I was traveling and lecturing less, I had more evenings free.

But this is all hindsight. I don't remember thinking, "My love life is shot, the work has gone to hell, and I have time on my hands, so I'm going to get a guitar to fill up the time and make me feel better." All of a sudden I wanted a guitar. For a while the idea seemed extravagant, as I still had very little money. Finally one day I walked into Schirmer's music store and asked what guitars cost. The man in the store said I could get one very cheap, but that it would not be much fun to play and might give trouble. He recommended a Martin, for one hundred dollars. He showed it to me. It looked lovely, sounded even better. I'll take it, I said, bought some little instruction book and a book of Burl Ives songs, gave him a check, and took the guitar home.

I loved that instrument. From the instruction book I learned how to make a few of the simpler chords. I spent much time just slowly strumming these chords, enjoying their rich, mellow sound, and the feeling of the guitar vibrating against me. Sometimes I would come home late at night from a committee or board meeting or a lecture, keyed up and agitated, in no mood for sleep. I would take out the guitar, look at it, admire the pretty, different-colored woods, hold it up to the light to make sure that the finish was unblemished, wipe off a fingerprint here and there, enjoy the look and smell and feel of it. Then I would play the few chords I knew, and the sound and vibrations were immensely relaxing and soothing. But I must insist, I was not playing the guitar *so that* I would be relaxed and soothed, ready for sleep, but because I loved to play it. It may well have been therapeutic, but only *because* I did not play it for therapy. The point is important; to take up music might help many people to solve, or better bear, their troubles—but *not* if they take it up only for that reason. To get any help or health from music (and I suspect, anything else), we must come to it for its own sake.

Along with the chords, I began to learn some of the songs in the Burl Ives book. I don't remember how I figured them out. Something in the instruction book must have told me how to find where the notes lay on the fingerboard. But since I did not figure out the meaning of key signatures, sharps and flats, until some years later, I must have simply played everything as if it was in the key of C. As this was a book for beginners, most of the songs would have been written in C, a few in F and G. By playing all the songs as if they were in C, I must have changed a few of them in slight but interesting ways. One of my favorites was "The Colorado Trail." Some time later I heard a recording of Burl Ives singing it, and thought, "That's

I Meet Beethoven

funny, he doesn't sing it the way it's written in his song book." It did not occur to me that *I* had sung it wrong. Actually, I liked my rather melancholy minor or modal version better than his (correct) version on the record. "Why did he change it?" I wondered.

The guitar made it easier for me to get to sleep, but it didn't keep me from waking up at three in the morning and staying awake until just before it was time to get up. I know now that my insides were giving me a frantic signal that it was time to quit my job and do something else. But I didn't know it then. I struggled along this way until one day in May. There had been a sudden shift of weather; after some damp and rainy days a polar front had moved in from the north. Perhaps because of the freshness of the air, I slept soundly and woke up refreshed and feeling wonderful, to see a bright blue sky and small white clouds blowing along in the breeze. A day for kites and balloons! Breakfast—delicious! Down into the subway, and around to the station at Fifty-seventh Street and Seventh Avenue. Up onto the street for the walk down to Fifty-second Street, where our office was. As I walked along, feeling better than I had in weeks, the orchestra in my mind, which plays a great deal of the time and over which I have very little control, began to play cheerful music. It was the tune that the horns have in the Scherzo of Beethoven's Third Symphony, the *Eroica*. As I strode along in time to it, I began to sing it out loud, and propelled by this joyous music I turned the corner of Fifty-second Street, walked to the door of our building, went up the stairs two at a time, opened the office door, and went in to what I thought of as my life work. The music died out, and after a second or two a voice, which seemed to come from somewhere else, but must have been my own, said, "Oh, God."

For a minute or more I stood in the door without moving, not really thinking, just hearing the echo of that voice. The music did not return, and to that voice there came no answer.

I Buy a Guitar

After a while I began to think, "Well, if, feeling as good as I did this morning, this is how I feel about this work, it's time to do something else." I left my job about a month later. During the summer I decided to go that autumn to Europe for what I thought would be three or four months, but turned out to be ten. I left the guitar with my sister Jane that summer, not wanting to take it with me—I was planning, among other things, to ride a bicycle from Paris to Rome. When I returned a year later and began to teach school in Colorado, I was too busy for the guitar, and when, a little later, one of my nephews began to play it, and quite well, I was glad to give it to him. For by then my musical life was beginning to turn in new directions.

The Szigeti Syndrome

In October 1952 I went by ship to England, stayed a few days with friends near Southampton, and then went to London for about six weeks. I spent a lot of time there with some young student teachers who were active in the Youth Section of the Labor Party. In between all this I walked all over London, saw the sights, and went to three concerts at the Royal Festival Hall.

The first of these was the Philharmonia Orchestra, then one of the great orchestras of the world, playing an all-Beethoven program—the Eighth Symphony, a piano concerto, and the Seventh Symphony. Concerts were much cheaper then in London than in New York, so I splurged on a good seat, about the center of the third row. I had never been so close to a symphony orchestra. Even more than when I heard *The Rite* in New York, I could see how much *effort* it took the players to make the music. To hear the Seventh, still my favorite of all symphonies, at such close range was thrilling. It was also very instructive. I could see as well as hear where the various notes, sounds, parts of the music, were coming from. I was beginning to learn what the various instruments looked and sounded like, how people played them, and where they were placed in the orchestra, so that later, listening to records, I could see and feel the orchestra as well as hear it. I began to sense what enormous coordination, teamwork, and discipline went into that music.

Later I heard a concert of the BBC Symphony. The first oboeist was a thin, dark-haired young woman who moved her head ever so slightly, but very intensely, as she played accented notes. Many great oboe players do not do this, and many might say that they should not—too much head bobbing could be an annoying distraction. In this case it did not distract me, but made me feel how deeply the player was involved in the music. Like many jazz musicians and jazz lovers, I was used to saying condescendingly that all classical musicians did was just play the notes. Here I could see, and not just in this oboeist, that this was not true at all, that at its best a great symphony orchestra plays with the same intensity and commitment that I had heard from the Herman band.

The third concert I looked forward to most of all. The main work was the Beethoven Violin Concerto, and Joseph Szigeti was to play it. After intermission the orchestra took their places, Szigeti and the conductor came out, there was the usual last-second tuning, and with the five soft strokes on the tympani we were off. As the beautiful orchestral introduction came to an end, Szigeti put his violin under his chin, raised the bow, and began to play. In only a very short time I realized with amazement and dismay that he was finding some of the rapid and intricate passages very difficult, playing with much roughness and strain, and making every now and then what even my untrained ear could hear were wrong notes. Wrong notes! Joseph Szigeti, one of the world's great violinists, up there in front of all these people, *making mistakes!* My face began to

The Szigeti Syndrome

grow hot and red with shame and embarrassment. I shrank in my seat, didn't want to look at anyone else. I could not have felt worse if Szigeti's pants had fallen down right on the stage. Projecting these feelings all over the Festival Hall, I assumed that every one of the three thousand people there was as ashamed as I was. Szigeti played on, in what was probably a very tough, thoughtful, and beautiful performance. But I could barely get past the wrong notes to hear the music. Even when he was not making mistakes, I was in an agony of suspense lest he make some. As the concert ended, I dreaded that the audience might burst out into laughter, or boos and hisses. But no, only applause. Hadn't they heard those mistakes? Still hardly wanting to look at anyone else, I left the hall and went home. An hour later I still felt some of that embarrassment and shame.

From time to time, over the years, I thought about that concert and my feelings, but not for a long time did I understand what my feelings were really about. I had supposed that I was feeling shame and embarrassment *for* Szigeti, sharing what he must have been feeling as he heard himself make mistakes. What I finally came to understand is that I was not thinking about him, not feeling for him at all, but imagining *myself* up there, making those mistakes, and imagining all those three thousand people sneering and laughing *at me.* What he may have thought about that concert, I will never know. He was near the end of his performing career—this must have been one of his last public appearances. He must have known very well, from his practicing and rehearsing, that the concerto would strain his resources to the very limit. Knowing this, he must have decided that he still had something to say about this beloved music, and wanted to say it in public one last time, even at the cost of making some mistakes. He took the risk, and at the end, probably judged that it was worth it —even behind the fog of my shame, I could hear moments of

I Meet Beethoven

great beauty, and intelligent listeners must have heard many more. To his friends, afterwards, he may have joked about some of the mistakes. But they were not important; what was important was making the music.

In much this spirit Arthur Rubinstein played many of his late concerts. To be sure, he missed some notes; he knew he was going to miss them; but the beauty and meaning of the music came through anyway. Of course, only after a long career of making great music does a performer earn the right to make mistakes in public and to have them overlooked or forgiven. No young player who had as much trouble with the Beethoven concerto as Szigeti did that night, would be asked or allowed to play it in public. But even the most technically skilled young players do not get up in front of an audience thinking about not making mistakes. They get up to play the music, to say to the audience whatever they think that music is trying to say. Had they feared their own mistakes as much as I feared Szigeti's at that concert, they never would have made it through their first recital. I was only to learn later how much of an obstacle this would be for me.

The Szigeti Syndrome

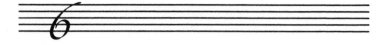

6

Solving a Mystery

Decoding the Sharps and Flats

I came back from Europe in August 1953, not knowing what to do next. My sister Jane urged me to teach school. I said it didn't interest me. But she persuaded me at least to visit the Colorado Rocky Mountain School, which had just opened in Carbondale, not far from Aspen. In early October I spent a day there, and liked it so much that I stayed and began teaching. It was a college preparatory boarding school, coeducational, which was then unusual, and still more unusual in that the students and faculty did almost all the manual work of the school, including much of the building and (later) some of the food raising. The school was very small, had only seventeen students in its first year, and in its fourth year (and my last) only sixty.

From the start we sang a lot. The school secretary played the guitar, knew a great many Western and other folk songs, and led a folk singing group. Anne Holden, the codirector, and another teacher started a small singing group, which I was happy to join as a tenor. At first just a few of us would gather from time to time and sing songs, rounds, and madrigals. After a while this informal singing became a regular activity, and the group was named the Madrigal Group. It kept this name for many years, even after it had become a full-fledged chorus. As at Exeter I learned my parts by heart from somebody who already knew them, and sang them from memory. I would have been glad to go on leaning on more experienced singers, but there were none to lean on. There was one other tenor, a student. I have often wondered what Arthur Landers would have made of him. He not only raised his eyebrows when he had to sing high notes, he actually bent way back and looked straight up at the ceiling, like a jazz trumpeter doing a hot lick. But he was slower to learn parts than I was, and was clearly planning to lean on me. So I had to become a leader.

This was easy enough, as long as we sang only a few short songs. But in the school's second year the Madrigal Group became more ambitious, wanted to be a regular chorus or glee club like the ones in bigger schools. Anne Holden, who accompanied on the piano, and the director decided to tackle some of the great choral music, including "The Heavens Are Telling the Glory of God," from Haydn's *The Creation,* and a number of choruses—"O Thou That Tellest Good Tidings to Zion," "For unto Us a Child Is Born," "Glory to God," and others, from Handel's *Messiah.* This posed a problem for me. The only people who knew enough about music to figure out my parts had no time to do it. I saw after a while that the only way I could get my parts was to use the book and figure them out for myself. I already knew, or found out from someone or something, the names of the written notes, and how to find them on the piano. But there remained the mystery of keys, key signatures, sharps and flats. I finally knew enough to know that these were important and could not be ignored, as I had done with the Burl Ives Song Book. Here and there I would hear or read that this song or that symphony was in the key of G, or D, or B-flat, or whatever. Clearly these had something to do with those little marks over at the left-hand side of the music page, and these in turn had something to do with how we sang the music. But what? Since no one had time to explain even that much music theory to me, I decided I would have to figure it out for myself.

Yet these words are not quite exact. I hadn't done as much figuring out then as I have by now, and wasn't as confident that I *could* figure things out. Closer to the truth to say I saw that here was a mystery I was going to have to look into further. One day I sat down at the piano and began to think about all this. I knew which of the keys were named C, and I think I knew that if music was in the key of C there were no sharps or flats in the key signature. Why weren't there? Beginning with C, I started to play all the white notes in rising order, and found that these made a major scale. Then I started with some other note, and found to my surprise that when I played the white notes in order, I did not get a major scale. What did I have to do, then, to get a major scale if I began with a note other than C? I think I had heard someone say that the key of G had only one sharp in it. So I began with G, played the white notes, and got a major scale—right up to the last note. That one came out wrong. To make the major scale I had to hit the black note just before G. I knew enough to know that this would be either F-sharp or G-flat. Why did they decide to call it F-sharp instead of G-flat? I may have puzzled over this quite a while, until I began to think about how we would write down that scale. I then saw that if we called that black note G-flat we would have two notes of the scale on the same space or line, and nothing in the space or line just below it—the scale would look funny on the paper. To make it look right, we would have to call that note an F-sharp. And then I realized that instead of putting the sharp sign after every F note we wrote, all we had to do was put one sharp sign on the F line or space, to tell us that every F we hit was going to be an F-sharp.

This mini-discovery was enormously exciting to me. To have what has always been a mystery suddenly turn into simple everyday common sense is more than satisfying—it is not straining language too far to call it ecstatic, even erotic. I wanted to shout, "Hey, everybody, come here, get this, listen to this!" Instead, I explored further. I picked another note to start with, played a major scale, noted what black keys I had to hit, figured out what they would be called. After a while I started writing this down. By the time I had made major scales for all the white notes, I could see that only one note, G, had one sharp in its scale; only one note, D, had two; only one note, A, had three; and so on. I also saw, then or perhaps later, that the F-sharp in the G scale is also in the D scale, the A scale, the E scale, and so on; and that the F-sharp and C-sharp in the D scale are both in the A, E, etc., scales, and so on. In other words, to go from a key signature of three sharps to one of four sharps, you just add one sharp to the three you already have; you don't have to scratch them out and start again. This made things somewhat simpler. I don't think I figured out until sometime later, when I began playing instruments, the patterns that the sharps (or flats) made; that is, if your first two sharps are F and C, the third one will be G (one after the F), the fourth will be D (one after the C), the fifth one will be A (one after the G), and so on. None of the music we sang was written in such complicated keys; it was only when I saw *all* the key signatures on one page, in flute or cello exercises, that I could see how those patterns went.

But (to return to that piano) there was a small mystery left. One white note, F, gave me a scale with no sharps in it, but one flat, B-flat. Odd. There must be other notes which would give scales with more flats in them. Since they weren't among the white notes, they must be among the black. So I began to play scales, beginning with the various black notes. Again I found that one and only one black note gave me a scale with two black notes in it; another black note, but still only one, gave a scale with three black notes in it, and so on. Each of these scales had its own pattern of black or flatted notes—and here I saw the reason for the term "key signature," which had never made sense to me. Looking a bit further, I found another interesting pattern. The key of F had one flat in its signature, B-flat. But B-flat had two flats in its signature, B-flat and E-flat. Did this mean that the key of E-flat would have three flats in its signature? Yes, it did, B-flat, E-flat, and A-flat. That meant the key of A-flat would have to have four flats in its signature, which indeed it did. More excitement, more wanting to shout, "Hey, look at this!"

After I had digested these discoveries for a while, I realized that any tune that was written down, I could now figure out for myself. I looked at the orange song book we were using, which until only a few hours before had been a closed book to me, and thought, "I can figure out my part, everyone's part, of any song in this book. I don't have to get someone else to teach me my part." Like the little kid for the first time tying his own shoes, I wanted to shout, "I can do it for myself!"

So, I did it for myself. Very slowly and clumsily, thinking, "Now let's see, the next note's a G, where is the G on the piano, here it is, what does it sound like . . . ?" I picked out my parts of the songs we were going to sing, slowly turned them from notes into music, learned them, sang them. I had not done any thinking about rhythmic notation; fortunately most of what we sang was rhythmically fairly simple, and where I was in doubt I listened to what Anne Holden was playing on the piano until the rhythm became clear. The music was as thrilling as it had been at Exeter. Sometimes almost too moving; at one point in the *Messiah* chorus, "O Thou That Tellest Good Tidings to Zion," there is a soft descending passage, "The glory of the Lord," just before the final triumphant "Is risen upon thee!" That bit always caught me; unless I steeled myself well in advance, I always found myself so choked up that I could not sing the final notes. If anything, singing in this little chorus was even more exciting than singing at Exeter, because I knew more about what I was doing, and could hear more in the music we were singing. It was also very demanding; some of the notes in those choruses went very high, particularly in the chorus from *The Creation*, and "Glory to God" from the *Messiah*. We never had more than one or two student tenors, and they could only barely make those notes, if they made them at all. It was up to me to sing the tenor part loud enough to be heard, and it was exciting to think I could. I had to learn, did learn, something about warming up my voice, and about using it. Whether my voice ever became good enough to meet the high standards of that college freshman glee club, I don't know, but it certainly improved.

My First Music Pupil

In the summer of 1955 I went to Europe. In the fall, as I was getting ready to drive back to Colorado, the parents of one of my students, Sam Piel, asked if I would drive him with me back to school. Sam and I were good friends, so I said I'd be delighted.

On the appointed day I picked him up, we loaded up my car, and started off. We had planned a leisurely trip, camping out on the way. It turned out not to be so leisurely. After some hours driving, the car began to make a strange knocking noise, what I later learned was called piston slap. I slowed to about forty miles per hour and drove on, not knowing quite what to do. The noise didn't get any worse, so we kept going. Whatever was wrong clearly couldn't be fixed without major engine work, which would have made us late for school. We decided to push on, going no faster than forty, and hope for the best. At that speed (and less going uphill) from New York to Colorado is a long trip. We drove long hours, and slept in the car, or outside right next to it. Both of us suffered from hay fever, at its worst at that time of year. So we had a small adventure. Along the way we talked about a million things, and became much closer friends.

The car held up okay, the noise didn't get any worse. On the last day of the trip Sam told me that he loved music, and wanted more than anything to be able to make music, but could not, because he was tone-deaf. He sang or tried to sing a song or two, and he was certainly much further from the tune, or any tune, than my father had ever been. He told me the usual sad stories about being first made to sing, and then made not to sing, at school. In the midst of all this I suddenly remembered for the first time in many years what Arthur Landers had said to us at school about tone-deafness, that there was no such thing, and that people who had not learned to coordinate voice with ear could be taught or helped to do this, by asking them to match with their voices notes played on a piano, and guiding them to the notes. Sam was very interested in this. I asked him if he would like to try it, right here in the car, using my voice instead of a piano. He said he would, so we began. I would sing a note and ask him to sing it. He would, of course, sing a different one. I would say, "Here's my note —aah—and here's yours—aah. Now come down (or up) to mine." He would try again, usually get a little closer. I would repeat mine, then his, then mine, then he would try again. I see now that I might have done better to *slide* my voice up or down from his note to mine, or even have him slide up or down until he reached my note, at which point I could have stopped him. But I didn't think of that until much later. However, at each try he would come closer to my note. Eventually he would

Solving a Mystery

match it, and for a while we would sing our notes together, to let him feel what it was like to sing the same note he was hearing. Then I would sing a new note, and we would start the process again. With each new note I sang, he came closer on his first try to matching it, and was able to match it with fewer tries. Finally he matched my note on the first try. Triumph! I was as excited and pleased as he was. I tried another note, and he matched that. I sang notes all over his range, he matched them all.

We still had a couple of hours left before we reached school, so I thought I would try to teach him the major scale. I began with a note, made that the *do,* and then sang *do-re* and asked him to do the same. After a few tries he could match my *do* and then sing the correct *do-re.* When we had that well established, I sang *do-re-mi.* Same story. By the time we had reached the school, he could match any note I sang and then, from that note, sing the first four notes of the major scale, *do-re-mi-fa.* Much encouraged by this, he began to study folk singing with the school secretary—by himself at first, as the sound of others singing made it hard for him to hear and feel his own voice, and threw him off. It occurs to me now, thinking of this, that at least some children who are quickly judged to be "tone-deaf" at school might be found to be perfectly capable of singing if they could sing by themselves. In time Sam became coordinated and confident enough to sing with others. He sang in the chorus, started to play the guitar, and soon after took up the cello, where he showed such promise that one of the leading cello teachers of New York told him that if he wanted to, he could probably be a professional musician. As it happens, medicine interested him more, though at college he still played the cello for his own pleasure.

Suzuki's work in Japan, where he and his helpers have taught thousands upon thousands of otherwise unselected four- and five-year-old children to play the violin with astonishing skill, and even more, this incident with Sam, makes me feel very strongly that musical talent, the ability to play a difficult instrument at high levels of skill, is not rare in the general population but is very widely distributed. If more people, or most people, do not become musical, the problem is not with lack of innate ability, but something else, probably many things, including the kind of music teaching they run up against. I am not in the least shaken from this view by whatever people might tell me about the results of standard tests of musical ability. In music, as in math, or reading, or writing, what tests test, and all they can test, is the ability to take tests, and above all, to overcome the anxiety that all of us feel when we are being judged and tested.

In this connection the writer Michael Rossman, in an article, "Music Lessons," in *New American Review* no. 18, has told an interesting story. When he was very young, first going to school, the tone-deaf label was slapped on him. For many years he believed it. But after a while he began to wonder. He listened to music, loved it, could tell one piece from another, liked one piece better than another. How could this be so if he were truly tone-deaf? Eventually, still half fearing that the label might be true, he began to play the flute. He found he made rapid progress, and soon became skillful. So the tone-deaf label was quite simply wrong. How had his kindergarten or first grade teacher made such a mistake? The answer is quite simple. She had, apparently, asked him to sing "high" and "low," or "higher" and "lower" notes, and little Michael, who could *hear* perfectly well, did not know what she meant *by these words.* Unless one knows, as no little children would, that high notes have a larger or "higher" frequency of vibrations than low ones, there is no inherent, apparent, obvious musical meaning in the words "high" or "low." One might as well speak of red and yellow, or square and triangular notes. If Michael's teacher had only said "This is what I call a 'high' note, and this is what I call a 'low' note," his problem would have been solved, the words would have been made meaningful. Since she didn't do this, Michael did what all little children (and indeed virtually all adults) do in such a situation. He began to make random and panicky guesses, meanwhile searching frantically for facial and other clues as to whether his guess was right. Perhaps with enough such guesses he might in time have picked up enough clues to figure out what she meant and wanted. But he wasn't given the time; the teacher, like most official testers and judgers of people, was in a hurry to make her judgments. So, on went the "tone-deaf" label.

It is not our proper business as teachers, certainly not music teachers, to make decisions and judgments about what people are or are not "capable" of doing. It *is* our proper business, above all in music, to try to find ways to help people do what they want to do. To this a more conventional music teacher, a believer in aptitude tests, might reply: "Suppose you, John, had never met Arthur Landers, had never heard anyone say what he said about tone-deafness, what would you have said to Sam if he had told you that he wanted to make music and then given his tuneless chant?" I don't know what I would have said then. I do know what I would say *now*. I would say, "Sam, it certainly doesn't *sound* as if you could sing a tune, and right now I don't know of any way to help. But maybe *someone* does. Keep looking, keep asking, keep working on the problem yourself. If you want to make music, don't let anybody tell you, and don't tell yourself, that it is totally impossible for you to do it."

Are there, then, no limits to the possible? Of course there are limits. But they are much further out than we think. How much further out is made most vividly and movingly clear in a recent story, "The Acorn People," by Ron Jones (available from Bantam Books, 666 5th Ave., New York, N.Y. 10019). It is about very severely physically handicapped children in a summer camp, and what they were able to do once they had the help of people who were interested in helping them do what they wanted to do instead of telling them all the reasons why they couldn't do it. One boy who had no arms or legs, just four little appendages at the corners of his trunk, learned to swim. Four other children, wheelchair cases, totally without the use of their legs, decided they wanted to climb to the top of a mountain that most of the other camp children had already climbed. They went up part of the way in their wheelchairs, but the last part of the climb, many hundreds of yards up a trail too narrow and steep for wheelchairs, they managed by sitting down, facing downhill, and hitching themselves up, a few inches at a time, with their arms. And there were many other such examples of handicapped children doing the "impossible."

Bach, Haydn, Mozart, and Others

On that same trip I brought back to school a record player I had bought in England. I began to buy recordings of my favorite pieces, and of some works I did not know. Always looking for violin concerti, I bought a recording of two by Mozart, liked them very much, bought his other violin concerti, liked all of them, and from there went on to try some of Beecham's recordings of the late symphonies. The first of these to catch my ear was no. 35, the *Haffner*. I loved its vigorous and cheerful beginning, and in the dormitory where I lived used to play it first thing in the morning, as waking-up music.

One of the few records my last New York roommate had owned was the Bach Concerto for Two Violins, and though I had played it only once or twice, there were bits of it I liked enough to want to try them again. So I bought a recording of that, and also of Bach's Concerti for Violin in A minor and E major. All of these I found very beautiful, but for many years

Solving a Mystery

they were the only music of Bach that I knew. My uncle Randall Davey had played for me some music by Vivaldi, which the Virtuosi de Roma were just beginning to make known in this country. I liked it and began to buy recordings by the Virtuosi of Vivaldi's music, as they appeared. I don't remember what introduced me to the music of Haydn. In those days very little of his music was recorded; until about 1955, when Hermann Scherchen recorded them for Westminster, there was no complete recording even of the twelve *Salomon* symphonies, let alone most of the others. I decided to splurge on that album, and liked the symphonies right away, especially no. 100, the *Military*. About that time I heard Dennis Brain's superb recording of the four horn concerti of Mozart. I also came to like his Thirty-ninth Symphony, and later, the Fortieth, now my favorite; but it was a long time before I liked the Forty-first, the *Jupiter*. As for Beethoven, I stayed for a while with what I knew, the Violin Concerto and Third, Fifth, Sixth, and Seventh symphonies. Later I began to buy the Toscanini recordings of some of the others. I bought a recording of the Brahms *Requiem*, which I loved as much as ever. Randall Davey played for me a recording of the Brahms Double Concerto; right away the initial theme grabbed my ear, and the return to it, after the first statements by the violin and the cello, was very exciting. But not for many years did I explore the Brahms symphonies. Nor did I look into any piano music whatever.

One other composer I remember getting to know in those years was Sibelius. In a magazine I saw an ad for very cheap records, three for five dollars. One was of the Sibelius Second Symphony, and as I had been curious about his music I took a chance. The first movement was strange; it made little impression on me at first. But the second movement had one of those mind-seizing moments, a slow descending figure on the brass, punctuated with great silences, music of great bleakness and sadness. From that beginning, the symphony captured me and made me want to hear more of his music, which I was able to do only when I went to Boston. I must have heard much other music as well—the school had some records of its own. But from this time on I began to hear and like so much music that with few exceptions I can no longer be sure when I first heard what. Classical music had me well hooked.

Trumpet in the Snow

Every year, about the first week in May, the whole school used to take a week-long Spring Trip. We would pack up rough and warm clothes, raingear, bedrolls and sleeping bags, and food for a week, load up our vehicles, which were two open trucks with benches in the back, a big carryall, and a couple of faculty station wagons, and head off for a week of exploring and camping in the many national parks and monuments in the Four Corners region—i.e., where New Mexico, Arizona, Colorado, and Utah meet. At night we would stop at campgrounds, then still uncrowded, divide up into cooking groups, cook and eat our suppers, and sleep on the ground under the sky. We carried no tents. There was—we hoped—no need for them; May is usually very dry in that country. In case of rain there were tarps which could be rigged to cover the trucks, and everyone had ponchos or slickers to keep themselves dry. So if a wet trip was less fun than a dry trip, it was still fun.

The trips were a great experience. The Four Corners country is like nothing else I or any of the others had seen: wide, open, bleak, colored in strange hues of red and brown, with even stranger formations of rocks and canyons, a place where human beings hardly belong, and where they are not very important. The rather closed-in mountain valley where the school was had seemed wild enough to us when we first saw it,

Solving a Mystery

106

but compared to these endless reaches of desert and near-desert, it seemed positively cozy. The monuments themselves, ruins of old Indian structures, were fascinating—Mesa Verde, above all Chaco Canyon, where Stone Age people had built of stones, without mortar, an immense communal dwelling that until the late nineteenth century was the largest apartment building in the U.S. In between we rode around in the trucks, looked, thought, daydreamed, slept, sang, joked and horsed around, and talked about everything. Even at school, relations between students and teachers were generally friendly and informal, but here much more so—unbounded by schedules and things-to-be-done, we had more space in our lives, and our truest natures could come out. They were very happy times.

In my fourth and last year at the school, some new teachers joined us, and two of them, Hugh and Joan McKay, became special friends of mine. Hugh was my assistant soccer coach. I took very seriously the idea of "grooming" him for the job, and wrote him letters about the team the year after I left, to which he replied with detailed reports of their (very good) season. He was also an exceedingly fine jazz trumpet player. When growing up, he had left his high-powered prep school to spend a year in the music business. He had been considered one of the most promising of the young jazz players, and had enjoyed it. But he had seen that the jazz music business was (then as now) a very difficult and often destructive way to live, and had thought it wiser to return to school, college, and, when I knew him, to working as a teacher. Once in a while he played his trumpet for us, and very well. We liked each other, had a similar sense of the humorous and absurd. One afternoon on the spring trip of that year we were driving slowly up a steep, winding road in Navajo country, when I saw by the road a little wooden sign that said, "Whoa." I pointed it out to him. He looked at it thoughtfully for about a second and then with a perfectly straight face explained, "Well, you see, the

Trumpet in the Snow

Indians couldn't read, so they taught their horses to read."

We had a fairly wet trip that year. On rainy nights we put the tarps over the trucks, and people slept in them. Others slept under the trucks, or in the carryall or station wagons. Still others, including Hugh and I, were able to rig some sort of shelter out of their ponchos. In that season even when it rained it didn't pour, and a little shelter was often enough. Our plan had been to come up from the south to Mesa Verde, go on from there to Durango for our last night of camping, and then drive over the spectacular Million Dollar Highway back to our valley and the school. On the way to Durango it grew colder and grayer, and as we pulled into the campground it began to snow fat, heavy, wet flakes. We were all tired, and ready for hot showers, regular beds, and creature comforts, so there was much griping and groaning. Part of the campground was covered with short juniper bushes, and Hugh suggested to me that if we joined forces, between the juniper bushes and our two ponchos we might be able to rig up a nice shelter. I agreed, and we soon created an architectural marvel, a snow-tight tent, less than three feet high at its highest point, and open at the bottom on all sides. Since it was an hour or more until time to start cooking dinner, we decided that we might as well crawl under the edges of the ponchos and into our new home, and make ourselves comfortable. In a few minutes there we were, in our sleeping bags, warm and dry. Looking out under the open sides of our shelter, we could see the fat flakes still falling, and hear the sounds of the school making camp. We felt indecently pleased with ourselves. Sheltered with such minimal materials, we felt that we had outwitted Nature.

And then, to make perfection even more perfect, after a while Hugh said, "I think I'll have a little music," fished around in his pack, brought out his trumpet case, took out his horn, blew through it a few times to warm it up, diddled the valves a little, and then put it up to his lips and began to play the great Bunny Berigan solo from "I Can't Get Started." I thought I would burst with happiness. Yet I felt some envy, too. How wonderful to have music at your command like that, to be able to say, "I think I'll have a little music," and to take out an instrument and *make* some. And I knew, too, that the whole school, milling around in the snow, was hearing that trumpet and thinking, "Boy, Hugh can really play that thing." I would have liked to have them thinking that about me.

But my envy of Hugh in no way spoiled my great joy in that moment. He played a bit more—perhaps thinking to himself, "I can't play this damn thing anymore"—and then put his trumpet away, and we just lay and talked. Next day—clear and lovely—we went back to school.

Concerts and Rehearsals in Aspen

After school was ended, graduation over, and good-byes said, I spent a few days hiking in the high wilderness country with another teacher who had a small cabin in a little ghost mining-town. Then I went to my sister Jane and her family for a long visit on a small cattle ranch they had just bought in the country above Woody Creek, about eight miles downriver from Aspen. It was a beautiful summer, and a wild one. There had been heavy snows in the mountains all through April and May, so that the mountains came into June with a heavy snow pack on them. It made lovely scenery; every morning, when I left the little cabin where I slept, a half mile or so above my sister's farmhouse, and started the walk downhill to the family and breakfast, I looked across the Roaring Fork Valley at range after range of mountaintops of the most dazzling white. But when the hot June sun began to hit all that snow, the water really ran. Little mountain creeks which ordinarily one could step across became deep, fast, and dangerous. The Roaring

Fork and Crystal Rivers, where ordinarily one could fish most of the stream in waders, or ride peacefully downstream in a kayak, began to look like the main stream of the Colorado. The Colorado itself, where it ran through narrow Glenwood Canyon, was deafening to hear and terrifying to see. I could not have imagined that water could look so destructive and malevolent. Except for the spray it hardly looked like water at all, more like some strange sort of metal. People would give themselves gooseflesh by saying, "Suppose we fell into that," and shuddering; it was like imagining oneself falling into a blast furnace. A couple of local daredevils earned temporary fame by trying to run Glenwood Canyon in a rubber raft; no trace of them or the raft was ever found.

Down the Roaring Fork, at Basalt, where the river takes some big turns, wire nets full of rocks were hung over the banks to prevent them washing out, and there was much worry about the highway bridges going. But danger never quite became disaster, the rivers rose so far and no farther, the roads and bridges held, and slowly things went back to normal and the valley settled into its summer routine. On the ranch, I helped my brother-in-law by cutting and raking alfalfa hay in the small, sloping, uneven fields that make up a mountain valley ranch. Bumping and jouncing around those fields on the tractor, my mind half on the cutter bar or rake and half on a million other things, heated by the summer sun and cooled by the dry mountain air, seeing at every turn the high mountains across the valley, I was happier than I had ever been.

In between times we went into Aspen to shop, to swim at a big pool, and most fun of all, to go to the concerts of the Aspen Music Festival, then under the direction of Izler Solomon, a wonderful conductor and musician. Then as now, the concerts were held in a big tent, but in those days the tent was smaller and the whole music festival, like the town itself, much less rich and elaborate, much more informal. In those days

Solving a Mystery

most people in Aspen were not particularly stylish or wealthy, and the summer musicians fitted easily and naturally into this easygoing community. Walking through the dusty streets of the town, one heard everywhere through open windows the sounds of musicians practicing—pianos, voices, trumpets, flutes. They were among the sounds of Aspen summer. Some of the concerts were chamber music. Once, with Hugh McKay, I heard for the first time one of Bach's Brandenburg Concertos. At the end of it Hugh said reverently, more to himself than to me or anyone else, "Man, they were such swinging cats!" He was dead right; Bach's music—as I write I hear in my mind the last movement of the Third Brandenburg, or the last movement of the Concerto for Two Violins —often swings as hard as the best of Basie. Another day, perhaps that summer, perhaps another—at one of the big concerts, with Solomon conducting the full orchestra, I heard Zara Nelsova play Bloch's *Schelomo*, which, then as now, I found greatly moving.

But the most interesting thing I did that summer, musically, was to go to some orchestra rehearsals. The orchestra rehearsed in the main tent, in the middle of a big open field. People could stroll in and listen to as much of the rehearsal as they wanted. I went two or three times. The first thing that interested and excited me was just to see the players coming in, driving or bicycling or walking, wearing ordinary clothes, talking to each other as they took out their instruments and warmed up. What happens at most concerts puts a great distance between the audience and the music. The musicians and conductor come on stage, wearing clothes that no one else wears anymore, and, without saying a word, play the music and then disappear. They might have come from another planet. Most concertgoers are used to this, and don't mind it; many even like it and insist on it. But this distance, this remoteness, may be one of the things about classical music that puts off many young people. It surely makes it harder for nonmusical people, as I was then, to imagine that they themselves might ever make music. But at these rehearsals, seeing the players arriving, getting ready, taking their places, the conductor talking to some of them, maybe discussing something in the score with this one or that one, brought me closer to the music, helped me to understand and even feel a small part of the music-making process.

At one rehearsal they were preparing the second symphony of Robert Kurka, a very gifted American composer who died in his thirties. Solomon believed in the piece, and played it often. Even at first hearing I liked it; many parts of it "penetrated the ear and stuck in the mind"; in my mind's ear I can hear much of it now as I write. It was a great help to hear parts of it played over many times; I was able to learn, and remember, and listen for, many things which might have slipped by if I had just heard it played once. When the orchestra ran into rough spots, and Solomon had to explain how a certain passage should be played, I could hear what he said, and when they played it again could often hear the difference. Watching and hearing the orchestra work, I learned by a tiny amount to listen to the music like a conductor, critically, to hear more of what was going on. Until then, I had tended to hear orchestral music as a great glob of gorgeous sound, concentrating mostly on whatever big tune was being played at the moment. Now I was beginning to hear more than one thing at a time—though how a conductor hears all of what is going on in a complicated score by, say, Strauss, is still something of a miracle to me.

At another concert they were preparing two works by Peter Mennin, a short piece called "Moby Dick," and the Sixth Symphony, a dark, brooding, powerful work that I would like to hear again. As before, hearing each movement, and many passages within a movement, played over many times, helped fix the piece in my mind. I began to listen, now and then, to see whether the players would remember to do something they had previously rehearsed. Usually they did, once in a while they did not. One such place sticks in memory. In the middle, slow movement of the symphony there is a short unaccompanied duet for flute and bassoon which ends in a moment of silence, before the whole orchestra starts to play again. At the end of this duet, the two instruments hold a note for two or three seconds, before they trail off together with a few very soft descending notes. The flute and bassoon were having a lot of trouble coming off that sustained note in unison (always hard to do), and Solomon had them do it a number of times, until they got it right. On concert day I listened carefully to see whether they would get it right again. They didn't! I found this reassuring; even these superhuman people could make mistakes.

In those days I knew nothing of conducting techniques, had only the vaguest idea of what the conductor was up there *for*. But in my listening I was much helped by the fact that in his beat, with his hands, Solomon gave the players a great deal of *preparatory* information, which I now know is the only kind that does the players any good. To see a conductor's left hand flash out just as the triangle player hits his triangle may look very impressive, but it didn't help that triangle player any. A great deal of what Solomon did with his hands told the players what was supposed to happen, *ahead of time,* and in telling them what to get ready to play he told me what to get ready to hear. Without knowing it, I was beginning to learn something about what goes into a piece of orchestral music, and how it fits together.

I remember vividly the moment at which I realized that playing musical instruments was not an act of superhuman or magical skill, but a perfectly ordinary and reasonable, if difficult, act that I could learn to do if I wanted.

At all these rehearsals and concerts, in a way I never had before, I began to look at the musicians and watch and think about what they were doing. Their hands moved quickly, easily, and mysteriously on the keys, or up and down the fingerboards of their instruments, almost as if they had a life of their own. Their instruments looked like part of their hands. The brass players handled their horns, trombones, even the tuba, as if they had no weight. Later, when I began to play the flute, I was surprised at how heavy and clumsy it felt. It was like holding a log of wood. For a long time I was afraid I would drop it. Only after a year or two did it begin to feel as light and comfortable, as *at home,* in my hands, as these musicians' instruments did in theirs.

By far the most mysterious of all were the strings. I could understand, to some degree, what the wind players were doing with their hands as they pushed down or let up their keys. But the fingerboards of the stringed instruments had no marks or frets of any kind, yet the players' hands and fingers flew up and down them and made notes just as much in tune as if they had keys. How in the world did they know where to put their fingers? The question haunted me. I thought about it at every concert, and between concerts as well. What they were doing seemed as magical, as superhuman, as jumping a hundred feet straight up in the air. I hated the thought that what they were doing was so far beyond my reach that I could not even begin to do it. Yet so it seemed.

All that pleasant summer I found myself more or less living with that question—how do they know where to put their

Solving a Mystery

fingers? One day I was walking along, whistling a little jazz, and I found myself remembering the day, many years before, when I had figured out what I did to make the notes of my whistling higher or lower. On that day I had gone from low notes to high notes and back, trying to be aware of what was happening in my mouth. I soon realized that when I whistled a high note I brought the end of my tongue very close up behind my lips, while for a low note I drew my tongue back and down in my mouth. Perhaps then, perhaps later, I realized that by doing this with my tongue I was making the resonant air cavity in my mouth smaller for high notes, larger for low ones. On this sunny Colorado day I did that again, low note, high note, low note, high note, feeling my tongue go back and forth. And suddenly a strange and unexpected thing happened. The question I had been asking myself all summer came to me in a new form. I say "came to me" because I did not, so to speak, *think up* the question; it simply appeared in my mind, as if a voice not my own had asked it. What the voice said was, "When you whistle, and you want to get a certain note, how do you know where to put your tongue?"

I considered this for a moment, and then thought or said to myself, "Well, I don't 'know where' to put it, I don't think about where to put it, I just put it there, it goes where it's meant to go, and the note comes out."

For a second or two this reply hung in the air. Then another thought followed it. A voice, but this time *my* voice, said in my mind, or I may even have spoken it out loud, *"But that's how they know where to put their fingers!"*

There was the answer.

For I don't know how long, I walked about in an ecstasy of knowing. I kept thinking, or saying, "So *that's* how they do it! So *that's* how they do it!" Words can barely describe how I felt. Many years later, and after many tellings and retellings, just recalling the moment, and typing these words on the

So That's How They Do It!

115

typewriter, gives me a shiver. It was as if a great door had opened to me.

I thought about my whistling again. How *did* my tongue know where to go to get a certain note? I remembered learning to whistle, as a little boy, pursing up my lips until they felt the way I thought they ought to look, blowing a stream of air through them, soundless, no trace of a sound, trying, trying, one day getting a faint ghost of a sound, trying again and again, the sound getting stronger and stronger, until there it was, a note. *One* note. How did I then think about changing that note? How did I get to be a good whistler? I don't know. I don't remember doing much whistling when I was eight, or nine, or ten; I can't remember any tunes that I liked enough to want to whistle. Somewhere, sometime, I must have whistled notes many times, shifting my tongue around till I got the note I wanted. Trial and error; feedback; satisfaction, *pleasure* when it came out right. And so in time the tongue learned where to go. And so, in the same way, the fingers could learn.

It would not be easy. The thought came to me, perhaps a little later, that if music was much less impossible than I had thought, it was much more difficult. I had thought of it as being like jumping a hundred feet straight in the air, or flying like a bird, easy enough if you happened to be a bird, but otherwise something that you could not do no matter how hard you tried. Now I thought of it as something like climbing a huge mountain, or walking ten thousand miles—difficult, arduous, painful even, but something that anyone could do who really wanted to do it, that *I* could do if I wanted. Soon I decided that this was exactly what I did want.

I Start on the Flute

One day not long after this I wrote Randall Davey, who knew many skilled musicians, told him I wanted to learn to play one of the instruments of the classical orchestra, and asked which he thought would be best. He wrote back that he was glad to hear it, and would ask his musical friends. After a while he wrote again to say that most of the people he asked recommended the flute; it was easy to carry, easier to play than most of the others, made a pretty sound, had much good music written for it, and could play violin parts on string quartet music. He also said that he had found a woman in Albuquerque, a flute teacher, who had a good flute and wanted to sell it. I wrote back to say I would buy it when I came down to Santa Fe for a short visit before going East.

When I arrived, Randall and I called up the owner of the flute, made an appointment, and drove down together to see her. The flute was a fine one, a Haynes, and the price about a third of what one would pay today. I wrote out a check, and the woman gave me the flute, and a fingering chart showing me where to put my fingers to make the various notes. Then she showed me how to put the flute together, how to hold it, and how to take it apart, clean it, and put it back in its case. I thanked her very much, she wished me good luck, and Randall and I drove back to Santa Fe. I was as pleased, excited, and nervous as a kid with a new bicycle. As soon as we were home I took out the fingering chart and went to work. I had more than once made a musical tone by blowing across the top of a pop bottle, so I was soon able to make notes come out of my flute. Not very strong or beautiful notes, but notes. Over the next few days I learned to make the notes of the chromatic scale, over most of the three octaves which are the flute's range; the very lowest and highest notes, I could not quite make. In between playing, I carefully cleaned and shined up the flute, leaving no slightest hint of fingerprint. Aside from the music it makes, just as an object, a piece of sculpture, it is (like all musical instruments) a lovely thing. In the next few days I spent many happy moments just looking at it, admiring it. Then I drove back to Colorado, picked up all my stuff at the school, and headed east to Boston, my new home, and, though I never would have guessed it then, what was to be my home for at least the next twenty years.

7

First Attempts

Good-bye to Colorado

After four happy years I left the school in Colorado, for several reasons. In a small boarding school without much money there is always twice as much work to do as people or time to do it. I was always rushing from this activity to that, scrambling to get ready for a class, trying to get papers corrected, to catch up. I never had time to think as much as I wanted to about my teaching and my students. Also, I had come to understand at least this much about failure in school: the students weren't learning what I was trying to teach them, mostly because they were convinced they couldn't. I had tried to convince them that they weren't stupid, with no success at all. So I thought that maybe if I could work somewhere with younger children, and catch them before they had begun to think of themselves as stupid, I might be able to keep them from learning to think that way.

Beyond that there was my interest in music. Not only was there no time at school for me to study music, but no one to study with, or people to play with. During the two months of the Aspen Music Festival, there was music in the valley; for the rest of the year there was almost none. So I felt I needed to live in or near a fairly big city. My going to Boston was almost a matter of chance. I had never lived there, or wanted to. But a very good friend of mine had lived there for a number of years, in a basement apartment at the foot of Beacon Hill. I had visited him and his wife for a couple of days, and had said I was going to leave Colorado to live in a city, but hadn't decided which one. He said, "We're going to Africa for two years next fall. Why don't you take over this apartment? Boston is a nice town, this is a nice neighborhood, and you can't beat the rent." I thought, What the heck, and said okay. Twenty years later I own that apartment. Boston has become my home.

One thing I remember about leaving Colorado. East of Denver, about sundown, I drove into the tail of a huge thunderstorm. After a while the rain stopped. The sun in the west was down behind the distant front range of the Rockies. All around me, as far as I could see, were the clouds of the recent thunderstorm, low, thick, unbroken, almost black in the fading light. But eastward a great hole had opened up in the blackness, and through that hole I could see an immense cloud, its towering sides a dazzling white in the light of the western sun. Toward the west, between the tops of the distant mountains and the dark clouds over them, was a very narrow strip of sky. Against this the mountains stood in black silhouette. But the setting sun had turned the edges of that silhouette a brilliant orange red, as if huge fires were burning behind it. For a long time I stood by the side of the road looking now at the shining cloud through the hole in the black sky, now at the flame-tipped mountains in the west, while a cold wind, the first breath of winter, blew across the Colorado plains. Slowly the mountaintops grew a deeper red, the light dimmed and died

First Attempts

out, the hole in the black clouds began to close up, and I began to shiver in the wind. I got back in the car, drove over a small rise; the mountains disappeared behind me, and I went on toward the east.

First Flute Lessons

In Boston I unpacked, settled in, explored the neighborhood, began the adventure of living in a new place. Slowly, like a transplanted tree, I began to put out feelers, new roots. From someone I heard about the New England Conservatory of Music, and arranged with them to take flute lessons. Came the day for the first lesson; I found the building, went inside, feeling much less like a grown-up man than a ten-year-old late for school. I timidly asked where the classroom was, found my way to it, knocked on the door, went in, and there met my first teacher, Bill Grass. He was (still is) a very friendly, pleasant, easygoing, good natured man, just the person I needed to help start me off on this journey of exploration and adventure. We introduced ourselves, he asked me a few questions about myself and my musical background, and we talked a bit. Soon I felt at ease. He asked me to play a scale. I played it as I had been playing it by myself, as a collection of notes, none having anything to do with any other. Bill said, more or less, "Well, that's all right, you can play the notes. But there are big holes between the notes. Now try to make the notes longer, make each note join into the next, make them sound like a piece of music." This idea of legato playing, of making everything, even scales, sound like music (which they are) was one of the first things Bill had me work on.

Another good thing about his teaching was that from the beginning he had me work on real music, good music. He did have me get an exercise book, by Taffenel and Gaubert, with the impressive title, *Grands Exercices Journaliers de Méca-nisme*, rather lamely translated "Big Daily Finger Exercises." The first piece we worked on was a Handel sonata, first the slow movement, then the quicker last movement. Soon after that he had me start on a much bigger piece, the Suite for Flute and Strings in A minor by Telemann, a famous and very lovely work. Later he had me buy another book of flute music, including the Suite for Flute and Strings from the Four Suites of J.S. Bach, one of the Mozart flute concerti, and the solo from Debussy's *Afternoon of a Faun,* all of which I began work on. It was hard for me, but the beauty of the music made it well worth it. The Bach I particularly loved. Late in the first movement the flute has a long solo, against an accompaniment by the strings (or piano), and some of the harmonic progressions in that solo were (to me) so unexpected and beautiful that I drew a huge exclamation point in the margin of the music. And the last movement of the Suite, a *badinerie,* which means about the same thing as *scherzo* or joke, is one of the lightest, gayest, most swinging little pieces in all of music. Even though I could only play it at about half or maybe even one third of the proper tempo, I loved it.

As much as I loved this music, my chief interest was still teaching. During the fall of 1957 I lived on money I had saved when in the Navy, and tried to write a book about my four years of teaching in Colorado. But before I could finish it, my ideas about teaching began to change, so much that most of what I had written soon became completely out of date. Early in 1958 I began to visit regularly the fifth grade classes of a teacher, Bill Hull, who like me was not satisfied with the conventional explanations of children's failure in school (they are dumb, lazy, or screwed up), and wanted to find out the real causes of their troubles and what to do about them. At first I only watched him teach, and later talked with him about what he was doing. Gradually, as he and the children came to know me better, he began to ask me to do more of the teaching. By the end of that year, and all through the next, we shared the teaching more or less equally, and then after school talked about what we and the children had done. Often at night I would write long letters to him, continuing these talks, or telling him new ideas as they came to me. Many of these letters later became part of my first book, *How Children Fail.*

This work, and these new and challenging insights and ideas, began to take my time and attention away from music and the flute. But in the winter and spring of 1958 I had time to work hard on the flute, and I think Bill Grass was pleased with my progress. I know I was; it is always exciting to do something better, to feel one's nerves and muscles growing quicker and more skillful. I began to feel in my lips muscles that I hadn't known existed. Sometimes, after a long practice, when I could control more finely and accurately the air going from my lips into the instrument, I felt as if my lips, instead of being soft and round, were as sharp and pointed as a bird's beak. The instrument began to feel more at home in my hands. One thing Bill taught me, to keep me from pressing the flute too hard against my lips, was to hold it with the right hand alone, balanced on the thumb, with only the little finger steadying it, and then bring the mouthpiece against my lips and blow a tone. It was a good teaching trick; holding the flute so, I could not put *any* pressure on my lips. But at first it seemed so unsteady that I only dared practice it over a bed or couch. In time and with practice it began to feel quite secure. Also, my tone slowly improved. Bill used to tell me to open my throat, as if I were singing. Sometimes, when my high notes sounded too thin and shrill, he would say, "Put a bubble in it." I half knew what he meant, though I didn't quite know how to do it.

Like many adults playing an instrument for the first time, I was terribly slow. I tended to read music, think about it, and

First Flute Lessons

react to it one note at a time. It was all but impossible for me either to read or play a group of notes as a unit, a single muscular act. Another reason I was slow, something I still have to struggle against when playing the cello, is that when I played each note something in my mind wanted to ask, "Was that note right?" and to be told, "Yes," before going on to the next. This self-correcting teacher in my mind was at times very useful, but I could never get him to shut up and get out of the way, all the more so since I was still very afraid of making mistakes. Sometimes Bill and I would play a little duet. I'd go along okay for a while, until I missed a note. Then I'd feel a flush of fear and shame, miss another note, feel my face getting red and hot, miss another, and before long I would come to a stop. Bill would say, "Keep going, don't worry about the mistakes, just keep playing," but as much as I liked and trusted him, I couldn't do it. It was frustrating for him not to be able to help me with this. And when I practiced, this constant worrying about whether the notes were right or not made me tense up, much more than I was aware of. The result was that after an hour or an hour and a half, just as I was really beginning to get going, I would have to stop, because my neck and shoulders had become so painfully tight and stiff. One of the things any beginner must learn is to be quickly aware of this kind of muscular tension, and to relax until it goes away. I can do it better now, and so can practice much longer at a stretch. But not then.

Bill did tell me one thing that helped me, then and even more now. Musicians speak of getting a piece into their fingers, so that the fingers know what to do without the conscious directing mind having to tell them. Unless one can do this one cannot play anything quickly. I found this very hard. My fingers kept forgetting. Bill used to say, "Vary the articulations," meaning, play them two notes in a breath, or three, or four, play them long and short, change them in other ways.

First Attempts

124

Once the fingers have learned to hit the correct keys no matter what the lips and breath are doing, they will remember. This is perhaps even more helpful on a stringed instrument, as one can bow in more different ways than one can breathe. He also told me to do something I now do often, which is to take a piece of music and hum aloud (or tap) the rhythm. In this way I can get the rhythmic feel of a piece before actually trying to play the notes. But I didn't do that when I was playing the flute. And it led once to a strange small adventure of the mind.

Telemann on the Bus

For some weeks I had been slogging my way through the first movement of the Telemann suite, one note at a time. The movement is written in 12:8 time, what in music is called "compound" time. In compound time (which may also be 3:8; 6:8, or 9:8 time) three eighth-notes are combined to make one beat, so that in a measure of 3:8 music, there is one beat; in a measure of 6:8, two; and in that movement of the Telemann, four. Though Bill may often have told me that, I didn't understand him, and went on ponderously counting twelve beats to each measure, which took all the life and bounce out of the music. I had no idea at all of what the piece sounded like. I had never heard Bill play it, had never heard a record of it, had never tried to sing or whistle it for myself. It was just black notes on white paper.

One weekend I went down to visit my parents in Rhode Island. I got on the bus for New Bedford and, as we drove along, looked out the window, thought about this and that, and enjoyed the music which my private radio or orchestra was playing inside my head. This mental music maker plays much of the time, whenever or whatever it wants. On this bus ride it was playing a tune that I couldn't place, couldn't even remember having heard before. I did what I always do when this happens, tried to guess, roughly, when the music was written, then quickly ran through all the music I knew from that period. Usually this works, though one day years later the music maker tricked me for several anxious hours by playing for me part of the Debussy String Quartet, but as if it were a piece for full orchestra. This day, on the bus, I went through my still limited repertory of music. It wasn't from any Bach I knew, nor Haydn, nor Mozart, nor anything else I could think of. The tune played on, and after a while I decided to relax and enjoy it. I had stopped wondering what the tune was, was hardly paying any more attention to it, when suddenly a voice inside my mind said, "Hey! It's the Telemann! It's that flute piece you're supposed to be playing!" My first thought was, "No, it can't be that, I'm not playing anything like that!" But soon I realized that the sluggish tune I had been playing and this dancing music in my head were in fact one and the same. I thought in amazement, "So that's what it's supposed to sound like." Clearly the unconscious musician in me, a better musician than the conscious, hearing the Telemann that I was playing on my flute, said, "No, no, that *can't* be what that piece is supposed to sound like," and decided for itself how it *had* to sound.

Playing for (and with) Others

In the spring of 1958 a teacher in the school who played French horn asked me if I would like to join him and some friends in a woodwind quintet. I said I would, and we set a date. I forget what we played—it must have been easy, or I couldn't have read and played it. It wasn't one of those disasters—of which more later—in which I got in way over my head and couldn't play anything. I would have remembered that. But neither was it one of those joyous occasions from which I got a message telling me that *this* was what I had to do. We talked about playing together again, and I was ready to. But the many problems of the ten-year-olds in my class, most of them as frightened and defeated, as locked into habits of failure as any teenagers I had known in Colorado, filled up my mind. I also played once or twice in rehearsals of the school orchestra. The conductor was a jolly man, a local conductor and composer, good at putting nervous beginners at their ease. I was not too scared to play, but too scared to have much fun. I had no sense of playing *with* the orchestra, of helping them make the music, of being a part of what we were all doing. I could only think about not making mistakes. So when for lack of time I gave up the orchestra, I did so without much regret.

Near the end of May, as I had said I would, I left the school to drive to Colorado and visit the Rocky Mountain School. I wanted to see the students I had taught the year before, find out what their year had been like and what they were going to do next. I took my flute with me, thinking I might play for the students the first movement of the Telemann suite, if I could find a pianist to play with me. This was easy; the school had a new music director, a wonderful musician named Ted Rickard, who in years to come, in that very small school, would teach his choral groups to sing music from which I think even Arthur Landers might have shrunk back—Britten, Stravinsky. Ted was a very good pianist; for him the Telemann piano part was about as hard as "Chopsticks." We got on well from the start. He understood how scared I was and did what he could to put me at ease.

Soon the time came; we went to the dining room; there before me were all the students and teachers, some old friends, some strangers. I tuned flute to piano, we agreed on a tempo (very slow), and began. I may have thought that I would become less fearful as I played, but not so. I didn't make very many mistakes, but at every one I was flooded with embarrassment and shame. I grew more and more tense, my face felt hot, my hands sweated so much I feared I would drop the flute, there was a kind of buzzing in my ears, I could hardly hear the piano. In a way, feeling great fear is like feeling great pain; it is like being inside a little box of one-way glass; others can see and hear you, but for you the world almost disappears. I lost almost all sense of the people around me. There was nothing in the world but me, my flute, the music in front of me, which I was hardly seeing—I was playing more from instinct and memory than anything else—and two arguing voices inside me, one saying "For Heaven's sake, stop, it's terrible, you're making a fool of yourself!" the other one saying, "No, no, don't stop, whatever happens, keep going, finish the piece!" The second voice won. I finished the piece. My eyes unblurred, the world reappeared around me, people were clapping politely. Ted, who was musician enough to know what I had been going through, was smiling encouragement at me. We shook hands, I thanked him, muttered, "Well, I got through it, anyway." He said that was very important. Which it is. Once you stand up to play a piece in front of other people, you have to finish it. No matter how bad your playing is, or how terrified and ashamed you may feel, you have to go on. If you can't play the piece *through*, however badly, before others, you will never learn to play it well. You can hope that each time you play you will be a little less afraid and will play a little better, and this may prove to be so. But that battle against fear and shame is never completely or finally won; it always takes some will power, some courage, to perform before others, and that is part of the excitement and pleasure.

Going back east later that summer, I decided to look up an old submarine buddy I hadn't seen since the end of the war. He lived in a small farm town in Iowa, not far from the highway I would be driving on. Not having money for motels, I drove straight through, sleeping now and then in the back of my little car. When I reached Iowa I called him for directions, and arrived at his house late on a hot summer night. The temperature was about ninety, the air heavy and sticky, without a breath of breeze. No one had air conditioning; people opened all their windows and lived in front of fans. My friend and I greeted each other, peeled down to shorts, got out some peach shortcake and beer, and began to talk. About 2 A.M. I mentioned my flute playing. He said, "Do you have it with you?" I said I did. He said, "Well, let's hear some of it." By this time we had had quite a few beers, so that seemed a fine idea. I took the flute out and played some of my pieces. After more talking, when it had cooled down a little, we went to bed. Next day I drove on east. Later he wrote me that some of his neighbors had asked him if he had heard someone playing the flute in the middle of the night. "Flute? Flute?" he'd said. "Who in the world would be playing the flute around here in the middle of the night?" They shook their heads, puzzled, saying they could have sworn they heard a flute. He said, "Maybe you dreamt it." For some weeks the Mystery of the Midnight Flute was the talk of the neighborhood. Whether he ever told them the truth, I never knew.

Later in the summer I went with an old friend, his ten-year-old son, and his son's best friend, on a canoeing and fishing trip in Canada, the first of many such trips. In later years, as the boys got bigger and hardier and could carry more, we would live in tents; for the first two years we lived in a little cabin on the edge of a small, wood-enclosed, and lovely little lake. I took the flute with me, and in the evenings after supper I would often sit on the cabin porch looking down at the lake below, and play a few tunes for it and any birds or other creatures who might be listening. My notes echoed back to me from the lake, the rocks on the other side, and the dense woods all around. Chamber music in a lovely chamber.

A Panic Scene

Back in Boston a few weeks later, I began taking flute lessons again, but my heart was less and less in it. I was now doing half the teaching in Bill Hull's class, and was also teaching math to the other fifth grade section. Every day Bill and I discovered something new about the children's thinking, some new tactic of evasion and self-defense. We talked for hours after school about what we might do about this, tried in every subject to invent materials that would make it harder for the children to coax right answers out of us, but would require them to do their own thinking. We had just heard about the Cuisenaire rods, and were excited by the idea of using them to make arithmetic (especially fractions) clearer. At faculty meetings most of the older teachers insisted we bear down harder on children, though every day in class I saw more evidence that most of the children were already too scared to learn or think. My mind was full of these matters. More and more, music got only the leftovers. When I went home at night I wrote long memos to Bill about the day's events in school, or designed or made new materials. Only when I was too tired to do this did I think about playing my flute, and then I was too tired to practice well, to challenge myself, or listen critically to what I was doing. I played mostly for relaxation. This was pleasant, but did not lead to much progress. My teacher was discouraged. In one lesson he said to me despairingly,

"You don't change!" A teacher myself, I know how he felt.

During one of my lessons I had a most strange, frightening, and revealing experience. The lesson was in the late afternoon. I had had a bad day in class, followed by a committee meeting full of bitter and angry argument. I was late in leaving, ran into heavy traffic, and arrived late for my lesson, with no chance to warm up. My teacher had also had a trying day, and was not his usual good-humored and patient self. He told me to play the piece I was supposed to have worked on, and was exasperated to find that I had made so little progress since the last lesson. As teachers too often do, he decided that by golly he was going to make me learn that piece whether I wanted to or not, and began to try by brute will power to force me to play it at the proper speed. I began to make mistakes; I wanted to stop and ask him to let me take it slower, but was afraid to. I began to feel as I had felt playing the Telemann in Colorado, but even more so. A pressure began to build up inside my head; it felt ready to burst. Some kind of noise, other than my own miserable playing, was in my ears. Suddenly something popped loose in my mind, and the written music before me lost all meaning. *All* meaning. It is hard to describe the experience, which lasted only a second or two. Strictly speaking, I could *see* the notes, I did not black out; but it was as if I could not see them. They were blurred, as if my eyes were refusing to focus. They also seemed to be moving about on the page. But above all else, they made me feel that I was seeing something I had never seen before, never heard of or even imagined. Those black and white marks in front of me were completely disconnected from all my previous experience. The word "disconnected" fits closely; I felt as if I were one of those old-fashioned telephone switchboards from which an angry operator has suddenly pulled out all the plugs.

These sensations were beyond all words unpleasant and terrifying. I could stand it no more than a second or two; then I

A Panic Scene

took the flute away from my lips and turned abruptly away from the music. My teacher understood that I had been driven (or had fallen) over the edge of something. He let me rest, tried to help me relax, and after a while we went on at a slower pace. I wrote about the experience in my book *How Children Fail.* Since then, quite a few professional musicians have told me that they have had exactly the same experience, at a lesson or rehearsal, working on a difficult piece under a bullying teacher or conductor. I began to suspect what I now feel sure of, that the trouble some children have in reading is caused, not by mysterious diseases or derangements in their nervous systems, which it is now the fashion to call "learning disabilities" or "minimal brain dysfunctions," but by just this kind of reaction to fear and tension, in short, not by "word blindness" so much as *fear* blindness.

Some years later George Dennison in his extraordinarily profound and moving book *The Lives of Children* gave this description of a twelve-year-old "nonreader":

> When I used to sit beside José and watch him struggling with printed words, I was always struck by the fact that he had such difficulty in even *seeing* them. I knew from medical reports that his eyes were all right. It was clear that his physical difficulties were the sign of a terrible conflict. On the one hand he did not *want* to see the words, did not want to focus his eyes on them, bend his head to them, and hold his head in place. On the other hand he wanted to learn to read again, and so he forced himself to perform these actions. But the conflict was visible. It was as if a barrier of smoked glass had been interposed between himself and the words: he moved his head here and there, squinted, widened his eyes, passed his hand across his forehead. The barrier, of course, consisted of the chronic emotions I have already mentioned: resentment, shame, self-contempt, etc., . . .

First Attempts

Clearly José was suffering from the same problem.

As I said earlier, I am playing these days in an amateur orchestra, with players much better than I am. Much of what we play, we play at least twice as fast as I could, even with practice. What I am slowly learning to do is to connect the notes played by the other cellists with the written notes in my part, so that when slower notes come along, I can join in. But this puts me under great tension; it is harder to follow all those notes that I cannot play than it would be to play them, and at the end of a rehearsal I am more tired than my fellow cellists. As I struggle to keep my place, voices argue in my mind. One says, "Ah, the hell with this, what's the use, you can't play this stuff, what are you doing here, anyway." My eyes want to slip a little out of focus, to skim over the notes without really trying to see them. Another voice says, "Come on, don't give up, hang in there, *look* at those notes, don't let them slide by, grab hold of them." And week by week I get a little better at hanging in there and grabbing hold of them, which is why I play with that orchestra. All the while, I have to struggle against the very feelings Dennison wrote about—resentment, shame, and self-contempt. How come those people can read that music and play it so fast? What's the matter with me, that I can't?

Not Ready Yet

In the fall of 1958 I took up my flute lessons again, but, as I have said, without much growth or progress. More and more of my time, thought, and energy went into thinking, talking, writing, and worrying about what my fifth-grade students were doing. At some time during the year I decided, much as I liked my teacher, to stop taking lessons. In the following years I still played the flute now and then, took it to school once in a while to play for the children, took it with me when I traveled, played now and then for friends. I enjoyed this. But I did no studying, learned no new music, did not try to play with other people, and never even considered taking up lessons again. I did not even think of doing this sometime in the future. It was as if that particular exploration of music had led me down a dead-end street. Why should this have been so, when I had been so eager to start playing? I can think of a number of reasons:

1) Much as I loved music in general and playing the flute in particular—and it was always a pleasure to take that pretty instrument out of its case and start playing it—it was still only a hobby, not at the center but at the edge of my life, not connected with any of my concerns about politics or the world or human life.

2) To some extent I was still not psychologically or emotionally ready to play a musical instrument. I was too frightened and ashamed of my mistakes, and the possibility of making mistakes, to be able to give myself wholly to the music.

3) The flute, at least at that time in my life, was probably the wrong instrument for me. It gave me no way to discharge in physical energy the tensions I felt in trying to play it. It was like my efforts to learn chess during my first year at the Colorado Rocky Mountain School. I was very competitive, hated to lose, still found in losing too many reasons to dislike a self that I was just beginning to be at home with. I could overcome this fear of losing, or at least keep from being paralyzed by it, in active sports where I used a lot of energy. But chess, a competitive and warlike game where I could do nothing but sit, was too much for me. Trying to think of all the possible moves, and all the bad things my opponent might do to me, my mind would freeze up in panic. It was no fun at all, and I soon gave it up. With the flute I had the same sort of problem. Compared to strings, piano, percussion, or brass, it

isn't a very *physical* instrument. All you do to play is blow gently and wiggle your fingers. My tension had no place to go.

4) I did not have a good enough mental model of what good flute playing sounded like. I had not started going to concerts in Boston and had no flute recordings. The only good flute playing I heard was when my teacher now and then played me a short passage to show how it should go. This was not enough to give me a standard against which I could compare and judge my own playing. Without such a standard I could not improve. I might have done better if I had bought or borrowed some recordings of great flutists, or had gone to some flute recitals at one of the local music schools. It might have helped, too, to make some tape recordings of my own playing which I could listen to later with more critical detachment.

5) I did not play enough with other people. This was partly because I didn't have time, and partly because, when I did try it, I was too nervous to have much fun. But some of this nervousness wears off with practice, and if my teacher had done more to get me to play with other inexperienced players, I might have learned to enjoy it more.

6) I was not independent or resourceful enough in my practice. I tried to do whatever my teacher told me, but I rarely thought of different ways to work on the problems he pointed out to me. Many things I now do on the cello, some invented by others, most by me, might have helped me a great deal with the flute. But I did not understand enough about what happens in our minds, nervous systems, and muscles when we learn music, to take an intelligent, critical, and imaginative part, the *leading* part, in that process. I was not yet ready to be at the center of my own learning. The time when I would be ready was to come sooner than I thought.

Not Ready Yet

More Exploring

Meanwhile I listened to recordings of more and more music. In Boston and Cambridge there were then many good classical record stores, run by people who knew and cared about classical music. Most of these had demonstration record players on which you could listen to a record to see if you liked it enough to buy it. There was also the record-lending department of the Boston Public Library, in a tiny room in the basement. They had a good collection, and added to it all the time. Each month they made a list of their new records. By filling out a card, a borrower could reserve one or more of these, and so hear them before they became worn, warped, or scratched. For many years after I came to Boston, the library collection was a great help and joy to me in my exploring. There I came to know and love more and more works of composers I already knew, and of others I had never heard of, such as Carl Nielsen and Albert Roussel.

Rush Seats at the Symphony

About two years after I came to Boston, I heard about rush seats at the Friday afternoon concerts of the Boston Symphony. The arrangement was this. At about noon on Friday afternoon people went to the Huntington Avenue lobby of Symphony Hall and formed a line. At about two o'clock, half an hour before concert time, the door to the hall was opened, we bought our tickets for sixty cents, a magnificent bargain, and went in. For many years these sixty-cent tickets were not numbered, and were for any seat in the back row along the sides of the second balcony, and also the three back rows at the end. Where you sat depended on how fast you could run, hence the name rush seats. (Later, to end the big rush, which

136

was hard on the old, they changed this system and let people choose their locations.) I soon found that I preferred the seats along the side, the closer to the stage the better; even if I couldn't see the whole stage, the sound was stronger and clearer.

Knowing about these rush seats didn't help me, as long as I was teaching on Friday afternoons. But in the fall of 1960 I began teaching fifth grade at another school, which to my great joy closed at Friday noon. Here was my chance. As soon as I had swept my students out the door, out I went after them, grabbed the next bus to Harvard Square, took the train to Park Street, changed to a Symphony train, all the while worrying, "Will I be too late?" Out of the train, up the stairs, into the lobby. Usually I made it. Once, when Leonard Bernstein was conducting, I was too late, the lobby doors were closed. Another time someone said to me, "I think we're all full, but I'm not sure, you can wait if you want." I decided to wait. I was two people away from the ticket window when they ran out of tickets. But most of the time I got in.

After a month or two of this the thought came to me that some of the children might like to hear the symphony. So I offered to take them, no more than three at a time. They had to bring enough money for their ticket, subway and bus fares, and lunch unless they brought one. I would take them to the concert and get them back to Harvard Square. That was all. I wasn't educating them; these concerts had nothing to do with school. I wasn't promising a good time; I said I wasn't sure they would like the music, but that like it or not they would have to sit still and quiet to the end, because I wasn't going to leave before then. About half the class took up my offer. Some went only once, some two or three times, a few a half-dozen times or more, and one boy, who had had no other music in his life, eighteen times (in two years). Of all the music he heard there, his favorite was Bruckner's Eighth Symphony—and why not,

Rush Seats at the Symphony

with all that splendid brass? In general, the children liked the big, noisy late romantic or modern pieces much more than the more classical ones—Mahler, Strauss, Stravinsky, Bartók rather than Haydn, Mozart, Beethoven. During these years I watched and listened intently, and grew in my inner eye and ear a clearer and stronger model of what classical music at its best looked and sounded like.

8

Beginning the Cello

Lessons

In about 1962 an old friend, one of whose children I had
taught, moved into a small house only a few blocks from where
I was teaching. Since two of her children were having school
problems, we used to talk about this quite often. Her house was
right on my way home from school, and I often stopped for
some talk and maybe a cup of tea. One day I noticed for the
first time a cello standing in a corner of the dining room. It was
there next time, and the next. One day when I arrived my
friend was busy outside and told me to make myself at home
for a while. I went in. There was the cello again, the bow beside
it. I felt a stronger and stronger urge to try it. After a while I
thought, "Why not?", sat down, took the cello between my
knees, and very tentatively and timidly rubbed the bow hairs
across one of the strings. The cello made a soft, low sound. I
moved the bow across another string. Different sound. And so
another time or two. I felt a bit like a kid sneaking into the
cookie jar. After a few more dabs at it, I went quietly back into

the living room. On a visit a few days later, I tried it again. This went on for a number of visits, until one day my friend said to me, "You seem to like playing that cello. It's not mine, it belongs to Hal Sproul. I was thinking of buying it and taking some lessons from him, but I don't have the time or the money. Do you want to buy it?" I said, "How much?" She said, "A hundred and twenty-five dollars." I now know that even then this was a very low price for a cello, even a student instrument. At the time, a hundred and twenty-five dollars seemed a lot of money, especially for something I had no real use for. I considered all this for about three seconds or so, with the mixture of shame and excitement we feel when we do something foolish. Then I said, "I'll take it." In a short while the cello was in my apartment.

For some months I didn't do much more with it than I had done at my friend's house. Though I liked the sounds it made, and the feeling of making them, I was still very busy with my work. But slowly the thought grew in my mind, "This is silly. You've bought it, why not learn to play it?" I considered this for a while. Start again on a musical instrument? Could I really learn to play one of the strings? What at first seemed both impossible and foolish began slowly to seem possible and not foolish at all. I had met Hal Sproul, and he seemed a very kindly and gentle older man. Studying with him might be rather nice. One day I decided, "I'll do it."

I was still working half-days at the school (without pay), helping the first-grade teachers with a reading method invented by Caleb Gattegno called "Words in Color," about which I was for a while very enthusiastic. Since Hal Sproul taught at his house, only a few blocks from the school, we arranged to have my lesson around noon. On lesson days I took the cello to school, where I sometimes played it a bit for the children, went to Hal's house for my lesson, and then went home. His house was small and cozy; we did our work in the

Beginning the Cello

living room, surrounded by reminders of daily and family life, comfortable old furniture, newspapers and magazines here and there, pictures of children and grandchildren on the tables. From the first second I felt right at home, as I had when I first climbed down into a submarine, or first saw the Colorado Rocky Mountain School. Every cell in me felt that interesting and pleasant things were going to happen here. As indeed they did.

I wish I had kept the kind of day-to-day notes about my lessons and my work on the cello that I had kept about my school classes, or about the learning of my infant niece. But it never occurred to me until recently that anyone else might be interested in how a forty-year-old adult learns a musical instrument. I can remember in a general way what studying with Hal was like, but only a few details of our work. My overall impression is of warmth and pleasure. Since then quite a few people who take music lessons have told me that they approach their weekly lesson with anxiety, even dread. It was never this way with me. My weekly lesson with Hal was one of the great joys of my life. I always looked forward to it, and was always sorry when it was over and I had to leave. He was a sweet man and a very sensitive musician. I suspect that as a cellist he was not a great technician, and not much interested in technique. What he knew, played, and loved was chamber music, from Bach to Brahms. He never talked to me about technique as such, only about the music we were working on. If he showed me something technical, how to make a slide or a change of position, how to bow a certain passage, it was always to make a certain passage sound more beautiful. His hands were broad, his fingers quite thick and heavy. His left hand did not look at all like the left hands of the great players. In comparison, it almost looked clumsy. But as he played, it seemed to caress the cello. And he brought a lovely sound from his instrument.

He might not have been the ideal teacher for would-be

virtuosos. He might not be (were he still alive) the right teacher for me today; though I cannot be sure of this, I am now more interested in technique than I think he was. But he was an ideal teacher for me then. He saw that for all my lack of musical knowledge, experience, or skill I loved music and was ready to fall in love with the cello, and that it was his task as my teacher to help me do it. How welcome he made me feel! It was always about midday when I arrived, so, though neither of us was a big lunch eater, we were always both a bit hungry. He baked wonderful whole-wheat bread, and often, when I came in, we would go into the kitchen and eat a slice of it, sometimes with a cup of soup, and talk about this or that before beginning work. For someone teaching eight students a day this might not be practical, but it does seem as if a nice way to start a music lesson would be to break a little bread, have a bite to eat together.

One of my earliest recollections of working with Hal is of playing a short duet with him, just a few notes. As we did a wonderful feeling spread through me. It seemed to say, "Yes, this is good, this is right, this is what you are supposed to do." I became aware of this feeling with surprise and delight, thought to myself, "But this isn't at all like playing duets with my flute teacher. Even though I liked him, I was nervous, now I'm not nervous at all, I *like* this." Some of the difference was in Hal, the house, the bread. But some was in me. What had changed?

I thought about this for some time before finding an answer. In six years of teaching young children I had learned that what they feel more than anything else in school is fear—of failing, of not pleasing, of looking stupid, of being criticized or mocked or despised or punished—and that this fear makes it all but impossible for them to learn what the teacher is trying to teach, or indeed anything at all. I had spent six years learning the many signs by which children show such fear, and trying to find ways to dodge it, or overcome or help them overcome it. I had had almost no success; fear and failure are hard habits to break. But six years of trying to free children of their Szigeti Syndrome had apparently, and without my knowing it, helped me to become much more free of my own. In short, I was ready for the cello in a way that I had not been ready for the flute.

Of our work together I remember a few details. The first music Hal told me to get was Book I of a cello method by Piatti. As musicians know but others may not, a "method" is a book of graded exercises. For beginners it is very useful. It gives them some simple tasks to work on, helps them get to know the instrument, and organizes their practice, until they know enough to begin to organize it for themselves. Piatti, like most string methods, began by having me play notes on the open strings, bowing first one then another, back and forth, until my right arm, hand, and the bow, knew where to "find" each string. It also started me playing simple scales, introduced me to the idea of left-hand positions, and after a while gave me short, simple pieces to play. It was a good beginning, and we followed it with Book II.

But Hal very wisely did not restrict me to methods for very long. He soon started me working on some of the movements of the first three of the Bach Unaccompanied Suites—the Prelude and Sarabande of the First, and then of the Second; then other movements of the First; the Sarabande and Gigue of the Second; the Sarabande, Bourrées and Gigue of the Third; and even, for a real adventure, the Sarabande of the Fifth. Of course, I could hardly play this music at all, let alone well, and many teachers for this reason would not have asked or even allowed me to play it. But Hal knew, in the first place, that in trying to play the Suites I would meet many of the technical problems that other students might meet in exercise books. More important, he knew that the beauty of the music would inspire me to work on these problems in a way that no exercise book could ever do. In the Minuet and (in the Baren-reiter edition) the Gigue of the Second Suite are some chords that require fiendish stretches of the left hand. Some of them I can't play to this day, but trying to play them has been a very good left-hand stretching exercise.

He also recommended *Daily Exercises*, by Feuillard. The title suggests that the serious cellist will whip through the book every few days, doing all the exercises. Perhaps experts can. I can't; the exercises are concentrated and difficult enough so that just doing one page, or a part of a page, can very easily take many hours. I don't find these exercises drudgery at all, but interesting, challenging, and satisfying. I could happily spend many hours every day working on them alone, and on many days I do. I am glad Hal introduced me to it; it seems much more compact and inclusive than many other books I have seen. But he never told me that I had to do this page or that page, or in any way told me how to use it. It was a reference book, to dip into as I felt the need.

We spent most of our time together working on whatever movements of the Bach I was learning, or, some time later, on the first and then the second movements of the lovely Brahms E-minor Sonata. We used the Schirmer edition of the Bach; it was cheap and there was no other he liked better. As I played this section or that he would stop me every so often to change a bowing or a fingering in the score, saying (like most musicians, as I have found) that the ways of editors were beyond him, what in the world could they be thinking of? I would play some more; he would stop me and correct me, showing me how it ought to be done, all this very easily and gently.

Later, when I began playing in an orchestra and string quartet, he would help me with any fingering and bowing problems I found in my parts. He was delighted that I was playing with other people, and, unlike many teachers, did not mind at all my spending practice time on quartet or orchestra parts rather

Beginning the Cello

144

than the piece I was doing for him. He made no attempt to teach me vibrato, and made no suggestions that I can recall about left-hand technique. I do remember him saying now and then that I should try to get more looseness and flexibility in my right wrist, and showing me what he meant; but he didn't talk about this often. What he talked about was playing musically and making a nice sound. One day I said to him that very often, in my practice, instead of doing this or that exercise or piece of music that I was supposed to be working on, I would just pick notes more or less at random and sit there bowing back and forth, for the sheer joy of hearing the sounds coming from the instrument. I said this a bit apologetically, as if I thought such fooling around was wasting time. Very wisely he said, "But that's the best thing you could possibly do. After all, the whole point of what we're doing is to make a lovely sound."

A Place to Play

One day, not long after I began taking lessons, I was practicing in my apartment when the phone rang. It was the elderly lady who lived above me. She said, "Mr. Holt, are you playing some sort of musical instrument?" I said I was playing the cello. She said, "Well, my husband is an invalid, and home all the time, and he says that he feels the vibrations of your cello in the floor." I said I was sorry and would do something about it. Her news surprised me; they had never said a word either about my flute playing or about my classical records, which I played quite loud. But apparently it was not so much the sound as the vibrations that bothered him. I thought some rubber matting under the cello and my chair might solve the problem, found a place in Cambridge that sold rubber mats, bought two of them, put chair and cello on them, and, thinking, "Well, I've solved the problem," began to practice again. Some days later

I saw the lady in the hall and she complained about the vibration again. I said I had bought some rubber mats hoping to cure it. But she said he could still feel it. Ignoring her veiled but definite hints that I should give up playing the cello altogether, I said I would try something else.

What to do next? I knew that by putting various kinds of sound-absorbent material on walls and ceilings one could deaden the sound in a room, and thought (mistakenly) that this would also cut down the amount of sound that went to other places. But having little money, I could not afford acoustical tiles or anything like that. I noticed that in my small bedroom there was a molding all around the ceiling. It occurred to me that I might hang from that molding, on picture hooks and coat hangers, all manner of towels, blankets, jackets, sweaters, coats, and other clothing. It looked very strange indeed, but it worked. At least, it deadened the sound within the room, much more than I would have thought possible. To walk in the room was a very strange *physical* sensation; the deadness of sound was almost something you could touch; it was like stepping into a big box of cotton wool. I thought, This should do it, all the more so since the bedroom was not under the living room of the people upstairs. With a feeling of relief I began eagerly to practice again. But soon the upstairs lady waylaid me in the hall with more complaints. There was now a strong hint in her voice that quite soon Drastic Steps Might Be Taken. Trying to be helpful, she asked whether I couldn't rent a little studio somewhere. Since she was rich, this seemed to her perfectly reasonable. For me, it was out of the question; it was all I could do to pay the apartment rent. But I didn't tell her that.

I left feeling irritated and troubled. At first it seemed unreasonable, in the middle of a noisy city, and only a few feet from the heavy traffic of the Storrow Drive, to make such a fuss about the vibrations of a cello. But soon I saw their point. To be old and sick, and have to sit in a chair all day long, is hard.

Beginning the Cello

For such a person even the faint vibration of a cello on the soles of your feet might soon seem intolerable. They might not be able to do anything about the traffic, but they could sure do something about me; they had been in the building longer, knew the landlord, and, most important of all, paid about three times as much rent. The vibration problem would have to be solved. Who could I talk to? I had heard about the acoustical firm of Bolt, Beranek, and Newman, then busy building Philharmonic Hall in New York. I called them up, told them my sound problem, and found myself talking to a pleasant and informed young man who quickly told me the hard facts of sonic life. To soundproof my apartment, or even one room of it, would be a huge and expensive job. Sound will go wherever air can go, so acoustically dead rooms have to be airtight. Sound also goes through walls—I still don't quite see how—and the only effective barrier to it is mass. I had two choices; either build what would be in effect a room within a room, acoustically insulated from the other, or put a very massive ceiling between myself and upstairs. I thanked him and gloomily hung up. No two ways about it; I could not practice where I lived. But where else?

On lesson days, when I took my cello to the school where I was still working part-time, I could get in an hour or so of practice after the children went home and before they closed the building. Even if I did this every day, I needed and wanted more practice time than that. A friend of mine, who taught Science part-time at the school, made a suggestion. He lived not far away, and behind his house was a small barn with a wood stove. If I wanted to come over and build up the fire myself, I could use the barn. I tried this for a while. It didn't work very well; if the night had been cool or cold, it took a long time for the barn to warm up enough so that I could even begin to play. It was hardly worth it; three hours or so of travel and barn warming every

A Place to Play

time I wanted to practice. I had to find something better.

One day a thought came to me. A good friend of mine taught at the Commonwealth School, a small secondary day school about a half mile away from me in Boston. I wrote him proposing a trade. If the school would let me use some part of the building for cello practice, before or after school hours, I would do something in return. I said I had taught secondary school, and could tutor kids in English or math or perhaps French. As an afterthought I said I had coached soccer and might help out somehow with that. This last suggestion rang the bell. My friend soon called me, full of excitement. The school, only six or seven years old, had a soccer program—it was their main fall sport for boys. But none of the teachers there had ever played much soccer or knew much about it. They were eager for an experienced coach. Soon we made a deal; I would coach, fall and spring, and in return I could practice at school. It was already October when we agreed on this. I began coaching right away. In two weeks or so we had a game, which we won, the first soccer victory in the school's short history. A good beginning.

With the school as a base I worked out a new practice routine, which I was to follow—at least, while I was in Boston —for the next two years. I would get up very early in the morning, between 4 and 5 A.M., dress, pack up cello, stand, and music, walk to the school, let myself in, go to whatever room I was using for practice, turn on a heater (the building was kept at 50 degrees F at night), and begin to play. At first I used the small gym for practice, then later a small faculty lounge. At eight thirty or so I would leave the school, go home, eat, sleep some more, do other kinds of work, come back after lunch for soccer practice, go home again for dinner, and then quite often come back to the school for more practice in the evening.

With this problem of practice space solved, I could really begin to work on the cello. On many days I would play four or five hours. I wanted to play more, but had to be careful not to overstrain my hands, above all the left. Now and then I would get carried away, play too long, and work my left hand until it became sore; then I would have to take it easy for a couple of days till it went back to normal. A further advantage of playing at school was that I was able to play with some of the students. One boy, a fine flutist, and I did some work on Beethoven duets. Another boy, a pianist, later worked with me on the first movement of the Brahms E-minor Sonata. All in all, my trade with the school was an ideal arrangement. It makes me realize, too, how difficult or impossible music making is for many city people who have complaining neighbors on all sides, and no friendly school, or any other place, to go to. Why should there not be some such places?

My First Cello Student

I had been studying the cello for less than a year when the friend from whom I had bought it said to me one day that her son, then about seven or eight, wanted me to give him cello lessons. I had known this boy since he was about four or five, and had come to know him quite well. He was a handsome, bright, energetic, passionate, angry, stubborn, and difficult child. At his best he could charm birds out of trees; at other times he could be impossible. His intelligent, sympathetic, and capable mother often found him very hard to deal with, and most other adults could not deal with him at all.

He loved music. He, his mother, and I often went together to the Friday afternoon concerts of the Boston Symphony. Along with two or three hundred others, we would meet early in the Huntington Avenue lobby of Symphony Hall, and wait there, talking, eating lunch, reading, knitting, or whatever, until someone began to pass out the rush-seat tickets for that afternoon, and to let us into the hall. On these occasions the boy was good company. He loved the music, and like most young children he loved being part of a serious grown-up gathering. Sitting there in the lobby, eating our lunch, we would talk about many things.

When the concert began, this ordinarily very energetic and restless child—who today would certainly be labeled "hyperactive"—would sit absolutely still and quiet, watching and listening with great concentration. We usually sat in the second balcony on the left side of the hall, from where we could see the cellists working away. And when the composer gave them a nice song to sing, which often happened, they made a splendid sound. So it was natural that when I started to play the cello, and appeared with it every week in his mother's house, he should begin to think of playing the cello, like me, and even of someday playing in a big orchestra, like the cellists we saw and heard every Friday. In this he was much like many other children who, seeing a fire truck, decide they want to be firemen.

Still, when his mother told me one day that he wanted to study with me, I was surprised. I said "For goodness sakes, I haven't even been studying a year myself, I'm barely a beginner. Why does he want to study with me?" His mother said, Yes, he knew I had just started. But he also knew that I knew more about the cello than he did, and so could help him. Beyond that, he knew that I was one of the few adults who could get along with him and work with him. So she insisted. Since I liked the boy, and since I liked the idea of helping someone else begin to play the instrument I loved so much myself, I agreed. We worked out a time and place, agreed on a fee, and the work began.

In agreeing, I made a few conditions. I insisted that playing the cello, and studying with me, be the boy's idea, not his mother's. He had to be free, and *to know that he was free*, to stop studying with me or stop playing altogether any time he felt like it, without having to feel ashamed or guilty. He had to be free to cancel a lesson if he wanted to. And I insisted that the whole matter of practice be left entirely up to him. Practice done in the spirit of why-do-I-have-to-do-this is worse than none at all. The only good practice is that done with zest and enthusiasm. I wanted this boy to play the cello for his own delight, to find out for himself that practice brought improvement, and to decide for himself how much improvement he was willing to pay for with work. His mother gladly agreed to this, and not only on principle. It was hard enough as it was to get him through an average day, without having to battle about practicing the cello.

At that time I had not even heard of Suzuki. But it seemed to me that the best way to begin, instead of having the boy do scales and exercises, was to show him right at the start how to play some tunes that he already knew. And it seemed a good idea to connect these tunes with the symphony orchestra he loved. So I picked two big symphony tunes, the theme from the last movement of Beethoven's Ninth Symphony, and the Andante, the "surprise" movement of Haydn's *Surprise* Symphony (no. 94). I then wrote these down so that they could be played on the cello in what is called the first position. This was a bit of a struggle, as I did not know how to write music, or transpose. But I worked it out on my own cello, then wrote each note down as I played it. Soon I gave him *his* music— two great themes from two great composers.

With this as our material we went to work. The first thing I wanted to teach him, the first thing every student needs to know, was how to tune his cello accurately. I found that the method of tuning I had invented for myself (of which more later) worked on his smaller cello, and was eager to show him how to do it. But his hands and fingers weren't strong enough to work the tuning pegs. What to do? Of course, I could tune his cello for him during a lesson, but what about when I wasn't there? No use practicing on a cello out of tune. He could, of course, ask his mother to tune it. But she might be busy, might say, "Can't do it right now, I'll do it later." "Later," however, is too late. The urge to work hard at something comes quickly and unexpectedly to children, and must be seized when it arrives. But his mother was divorced, working, with a house and three children to take care of. There was no way she could keep her son's cello tuned on demand.

Even if his mother had been able to take the time to keep his cello in tune, the boy, hearing her tune it, might have taken this as a kind of subtle hint that he ought to practice. Most children would probably feel the same. They are so used to being hinted at to do what adults want that they sometimes see hints where hints aren't meant at all. Some react by doing what is wanted, others by refusing to. One is as bad as the other.

Where children are made to practice, parents can tune their instruments before and during practice. (I have to retune my cello about every ten minutes.) But to tune a violin or cello accurately takes a better ear than many parents may have. In many families children may often be practicing on improperly tuned instruments. This won't help them and may hold them back.

We could make it possible for children to tune their own instruments by fitting these instruments with guitar-type geared tuning pegs rather than the conventional ones. Such geared pegs are of course used on bass viols; one sees them in symphony orchestras. I have asked musicians why such keys are never used on cellos. They usually say that they don't hold (neither do conventional pegs), or that they tend to buzz. But if they don't buzz on bass viols, why would they buzz on cellos —or violins or violas? Until recently I had never seen or heard a good cello with geared tuning keys. But (as I write this) the first cellist in my amateur orchestra uses such an instrument.

Beginning the Cello

She is a fine player, and her cello has a splendid voice. I asked her whether her tuning keys ever buzzed or slipped or in any other way gave her trouble, and she said they never did.

For that matter, the highest strings of violins and violas, and usually the top two strings of cellos, are fitted with little gadgets called fine tuners, with which the player can make very small tuning adjustments without turning the pegs. These are only used on the high strings, which are metal, because, designed as they are, they cannot be used on gut or gut-cored strings. Why can't we design a fine tuner that *can* be used with gut strings? Meanwhile, it would seem more sensible to fit all children's stringed instruments with guitar-type tuners, and I would recommend very strongly to parents that they do this.

At any rate, our lessons began with my tuning the boy's cello. Then I usually asked him to play a two-octave C-major scale. When he had the scale well in tune, and the bow moving freely across the strings, we would start to work on one of his pieces, whichever he chose. This sounds simpler than it was. Everything depended on how he felt. Some days he was full of energy and confidence. Playing his scale or his tunes, he would catch and correct most of his own mistakes. When I felt I had to make a correction in his bow grip, or bowing, or hand position, he would take it in good spirit. But at other times he was full of anger and despair, near rage or tears. At the very first note he would begin to criticize himself harshly. "That's terrible! I'll never be able to play this damn cello!" At such times my task was to give, not feedback or criticism or correction or advice, but reassurance and support. "It's OK, you're doing fine, you've made a lot of progress, it doesn't sound bad at all, take it easy, don't worry about a little mistake, I make them all the time, even the people in the Boston Symphony make them." And there were other stages in between, where he needed encouragement, but not much, or could take some criticism, but not much.

My First Cello Student

I could perhaps work with him more easily than others could because he reminded me so much of myself when I was little. Once when I was about eleven, and wild with rage after muffing several golf shots in a row, I pounded my favorite club on the ground till I broke it. Some years later, if I missed a number of shots in tennis, I would get furiously angry. I didn't break my racket, because I was quite sure that if I did I would not get a new one. But friends claim to have seen me once bite a tennis ball. I was, in short, a very bad sport. It was not so much that I couldn't stand losing as that I couldn't stand to play badly. Every bad shot I made seemed to me further proof that I was an all-around bad person. In the same way, for this boy every missed or weak or ugly note was just such proof.

So I had to pay close attention—and is not this true of all serious teaching?—not just to what my student was doing, but even more to how he was feeling. When he was feeling good I could drive him hard—no, that note's flat, that one's sharp, longer bow stroke, do it again, do it right. When he was feeling bad he would bleed at the touch of a feather. And these feelings would change, not just from one lesson to the next, but within a lesson. He might start a lesson feeling good, and later plunge into despair. Or he might start in despair, gradually gain confidence, and finish with a rush. More than once he went through the whole up-and-down cycle, all in the space of a forty-five-minute lesson. And he was utterly at the mercy of these feelings and powerless to change them.

In this way we continued. He did not practice a great deal, because he could stand to practice only when he was feeling good, which was rare enough—and then the cello had to be in tune, or his mother available to tune it. These conditions did not come about very often. But when he practiced he did so with great energy and enthusiasm. In any case he made good progress. His intonation became good, he began to get a good sound from the instrument, and he played his tunes with

Beginning the Cello

good rhythm and spirit. Soon he decided that he was ready, and eager, to take lessons from a *real* teacher. I was glad, as I knew he was ready to learn far more than I knew how to teach him.

So after a while he stopped studying with me and began to take lessons from a professional teacher—a good one. It was a disaster. The teacher had probably never known or worked with a child like this boy. He could not sense, did not understand, had no patience with the boy's rapidly changing feelings and moods, and could not or would not adjust his teaching to them. More often than not, the lessons turned into arguments and battles. Before long, the boy gave up not only the lessons, but the cello altogether. It had become just another source of trouble and pain in a life too full of them. Why, then, didn't he go back to studying with me? He would have seen it, quite rightly, as a going *back*, a kind of retreat. Sooner or later, he must have thought, if he was going to be a good player, he was going to have to take lessons from a real teacher and if these lessons were going to be a misery, what was the use of going on? So he quit.

I'm glad to say he did not give up music. Some years later he began to play the guitar. Like many other young people at the time, he began to sing folk songs, accompanying himself on the guitar. He had a beautiful voice, and was a fine and sensitive singer, might very well have made a career of it. On the guitar he was no mere strummer. One day, when he was about seventeen, I was at his house and heard him play a melody so sinuous, subtle, and hauntingly beautiful that I stopped what I was doing to ask him what song it was. He said it didn't have any name. I asked him where he had heard it. He said it was his own. I said, "Goodness! When did you write it?" He said, "I didn't write it, I just made it up." I said, "You mean, you made it up just now as you were playing, you never played it before?" He nodded Yes. I was absolutely thunderstruck.

My First Cello Student

Now, for the time being at least, his life has taken other turns. He lives in the country, in Maine, and is busy night and day with work that gives him little time for guitar playing or music of any kind. But I do not think that music, or even the cello, has seen or heard the last of him. I was in Maine a couple of summers ago, visiting his family, my cello with me. One day, when he was over at the house, he asked with a slightly shy smile if he could play my cello for a few minutes, just to see if he remembered anything of it. I said, "Sure, go ahead." It was soon clear that he had forgotten very little. His left hand soon found the correct positions on the fingerboard, he began to play in quite good tune, and with a good sound. He was clearly enjoying himself, and after a while looked up and said, "You know, I think I might take this up again someday." And I think he might.

A few years ago I was asked by the Music Educators National Conference, meeting in Boston, to give a keynote speech. When the time came, I surprised them by saying that I was not going to talk about teaching arithmetic or reading, but about music. I told them, among other things, the story of this boy, my one cello pupil. Then I said to them, "My credentials for talking about music teaching are modest, but real. The only person to whom I ever taught music *still loves music!* How many teachers can make that claim?" They laughed, as I had hoped they would. But I was serious. The question How many of my students still love music? is one that all music teachers might well ask themselves.

Two Orchestras and a Quartet

When I began to study the cello, I thought I would have about seven years of drudgery before I began to have any fun. But not so. Before I had studied for even a year, I had my first chance to play with other people. One evening I went to a concert at the New England Conservatory. At the end I applauded loudly. As we were all leaving the hall, a pleasant-looking, dark-haired woman said to me, "You seemed to enjoy the music." I said I thought it was gorgeous. She asked if I was a musician; I said I had only just started to play the cello. She said, "The cello! We need cellos!" said her name was Elizabeth Titus, and went on to ask me if I would like to play in a small chamber orchestra. I said I had just started to play and wasn't very good. She said, "Oh that doesn't make any difference. We don't play very hard music; come play with us." "Us" was a dozen or so strings, and a flute or two, who met every week or two at the Longy School of Music in Cambridge. They were about to play the Fourth Brandenburg Concerto of J.S. Bach. If I wanted to join them, I would be welcome. I said I would try it.

I bought the cello part to the Fourth Brandenburg and began to study it. With practice, I could play at least some of it. The evening of their next meeting I packed up cello, bow, and music, took the subway to Cambridge, walked to the Longy School, a comfy-looking Victorian building of dark-brown stone, found the room, and went in. Liz came over, welcomed me, and introduced me to the other players. There was the usual bustle of people taking instruments out of cases, tuning up, talking about what they had done since the last meeting. Feeling curious, eager, excited, and only a little nervous, I found my seat, introduced myself to the other cellist (fortunately a good player), and got ready to play.

Liz, a professional violinist, teacher, and coach, had organized this little orchestra. They played mostly music of Vivaldi, Corelli, and other Italians; of J.S. Bach; and now and then of Haydn—a year or so later we played his delightful Symphony no. 82, *The Bear.* As was the custom when most of this music was written, we did not use a conductor; the concertmaster, in this case Liz, gave whatever signals were needed. The flute gave us our A, we tuned again, looked at Liz. With a nod of her head she gave the upbeat, and away we went. At first I had nice, easy quarter notes to play, but I played them feeling much as I had felt when, bicycling into Italy many years before, I had spoken my first words in Italian—*to* an Italian. I half expected that the woman to whom I spoke would look at me uncomprehending, or perhaps burst out in hysterical laughter. Instead she understood. In much the same way I thought that my few quarter notes might be met with roars of laughter from the orchestra. But no; they were correct, the first cellist on my left was playing the same notes, they fitted in, they made sense. Like all the Brandenburgs, the Fourth is a wonderfully swinging piece ("Man, they were such swinging cats!"), and we two cellists were the rhythm section. A voice inside said, with amazement, "You're actually making music!" and then, more and more strongly, "Yes! Yes! This is what you're meant to do!"

Even in the Fourth Brandenburg there were quite a few notes that I played wrongly or not at all. I worried about them a little. But on the whole my feeling of surprised delight remained strong throughout the evening. And later evenings as well, though as I grew used to playing in the orchestra, the sharpness of those feelings wore off. But that was all right. I didn't feel any letdown. I had learned, and know even better now, that those ecstatic messages that tell us that we are doing what we love and need and ought to do, don't come every day. If we expect and insist on that much "reinforcement" *every* time we do something, we will never do anything. These messages come only once in a while. We must learn to trust them. Having been shown the road, we have to stay on it, at least for a while, even if it is sometimes a little hard.

After I had been playing with the orchestra for some months, Liz Titus asked if I would like to play in a string quartet that she was going to lead and coach. I hesitated. This seemed riskier than playing in the orchestra. There I had the first cellist to lean on, and sometimes another player, also much better than I was. I learned, slowly, when I came to notes I couldn't play, to listen to what they were playing, follow with my eyes the notes in my part, and play again when I came to easier notes. Still more slowly I learned, when I lost my place altogether, to look ahead to easier notes, hear when my colleagues began to play them, and join in again. Sometimes, when I was completely at sea, one of them would point to the proper notes in the part, or say "Two before D," or something like that. From them I could also hear when I had counted wrong and come in too late or too soon, and so correct myself. These are valuable performing skills, and the orchestra a good place, really the only place, to learn them.

But I could do none of this in a string quartet. No leaning or faking there. I would be the only cello; if I lost my place, no one could rescue me. It seemed a heavy responsibility. I said as much to Liz. She urged me on; one of the other players was not much better than I was, we would start with easy music, and who would worry about mistakes?—we could always stop and start over again. I said Okay, I would try it. Our first piece would be Mozart K.156. I bought the music, studied and practiced it. Soon we had our first meeting, at the home of our violist. I met the other two players, very pleasant and welcoming. We arranged our chairs and stands in the traditional square, tuned, and began. As in the Bach, I had easy notes to play, and as in the Bach, I could hear and feel right away how my part fit into the music, how it *helped*. It was even easier to hear this than in the orchestra; the other players were all close to me, the viola on my left, the second violin on my right, Liz directly opposite. Even more than in the orchestra I felt myself at the heart of the music. And once again I heard or felt, right down to my bones, a message that this was something I loved and was meant to do.

Two Orchestras and a Quartet

Much as I enjoyed the orchestra, I soon came to enjoy the quartet even more. I liked being solely responsible for the cello part. It made me feel I was really adding something to our music making. The music itself was wonderful. We played one or two early quartets of Mozart (though never the beautiful K. 157, which I and three friends are now working on). We struggled for a while with his Adagio and Fugue, a rich, dark, massive piece, which seemed to me less like Mozart than Bach (whom he greatly admired). We struggled even harder for a while with the first movement of the first of Beethoven's Op.18 Quartets, and learned how much harder Beethoven's music is than most of what went before it. But most of the time we played quartets of Haydn, a feast to last a lifetime. What a joy they were, and perfect for us; Liz could play well the hard first violin parts, and the rest of us could at least manage our much easier parts. At first we would be buried in our own parts, trying to play the notes, keep the count, and not make mistakes. But then, as we grew more sure of our own notes, we would gradually begin to hear all the other parts, and all the energy, surprises, and humor in the music. We would begin to play not just the notes but the music, and the quartet would begin to swing, as Haydn had meant it to. What a moment! It did not happen at every meeting, but when it did we would sit back afterwards and smile dazedly at each other, and say, "Wasn't that great?" as if four other musicians, and not just we, had done it.

Our host the violist and I were musically the two junior members of the group. He was a large and friendly man, with large feet. In moments of stress he thumped the floor emphatically but erratically with his right foot. I could ignore the sound of it, but that shiny rising and falling shoe was right in my field of vision, just under the edge of my music. I couldn't help seeing it, and sometimes the syncopation between it and the rest of the music would be too much for me. It became something of a quartet joke. We all knew we weren't *supposed* to beat time with our feet. I learned fairly soon to move my right big toe invisibly up and down inside my shoe. The violist would promise to quiet his foot, but in the heat of playing it would get away from him and begin to thump on its own. One evening I took action. I reached out with my left foot and very slowly forced the toe of his right foot down on the floor. For a second or two he went on playing without noticing. Then he began to realize that something about his foot felt funny, looked down to see what had happened to it, and saw my foot on top of it. We began to laugh; soon the others were laughing with us. Haydn was interrupted for a while, though I think he might have enjoyed the interruption.

One evening the violist's brother, a flutist, joined us to play a Mozart flute quartet. He too had a slightly unsteady sense of rhythm, and he too was a foot thumper. Instead of one rising and falling foot I now saw two, and not only were they quite often not in time with the music, they were often not in time with each other. One evening I said, "Gentlemen, if you are going to thump those feet on the floor, at least try to get them thumping together. When they get going independently it gets too complicated for me. Maybe if I were from West Africa, I could handle it; but I'm not." We laughed and struggled on. After a while we were marching, or playing, more or less, to the same drummer.

At about that time, through a friend in Boston, I found another orchestra to play with. Near where I live is an organization called the Harvard Musical Association. It has no present connection with Harvard, but was, I suppose, started by Harvard people. About every other week they have chamber-music concerts, often with very distinguished musicians. On alternate weeks they have what they call orchestra rehearsals. People come in, members of the Association and nonmembers, with their instruments, and under the direction of Chester Williams, for many years Dean of the New England Conservatory, they play various pieces out of the standard orchestra repertory. The orchestra is not rehearsing *for* anything, does not give concerts. It is simply a reading orchestra, playing for its own pleasure.

These orchestra rehearsals were interesting, but difficult. On the whole, the players were better than in Liz's orchestra, and the music harder. It was mostly basic repertory from the early or mid-nineteenth century, no problem for skilled musicians, but most of it much too hard for me. Sometimes, as in some movements of the Bizet Symphony in C, one of their favorites, I could catch most of the notes. Sometimes, as in one of the late Mozart symphonies, I could catch perhaps half of them. Quite often I could hardly catch any; I was not so much playing as constantly struggling just to find my place. At the end of a couple of hours of this, I was tense, sweaty, and exhausted, struggling against feelings of shame and discouragement. But it was good practice, if only at keeping cool under stress, and at training my eyes and my mind to move across the notes much faster than I had been used to. Slowly, in my half dozen or so meetings with that orchestra, I became better at this. I was sorry when I had to stop playing with them, and look forward to starting soon again.

Inventions

During these years, as I played, I invented some tricks that helped me, and might help others. The first had to do with tuning. It is both very important and very difficult for the beginning cellist (or any other string player) to keep the instrument accurately in tune. By that I mean that it should always be tuned to the same A—usually 440 cycles, the standard A tuning fork—and that the four strings should be exactly a fifth apart. (A fifth is the interval, the musical distance, from a *do* to the next highest *sol,* as in *do*-re-mi-fa-*sol.*) Tuning always to the same A may well improve the tone of the instrument. A cello (or other stringed instrument) is mostly a vibrating and resonating wooden box. This wood, being an organic substance, can change over time, and does change as the instrument is played. I often notice this in my own practicing. If I miss a few days, my cello is stiff and unresponsive. Even when I am playing it regularly it improves during a day's practice. The great cellist Gregor Piatigorsky said in his autobiography *Cellist* that on his travels he once came across a beautiful cello, which he bought. But it had not been played in a long time, and he said that he had to play it for an entire year before it was fit to be taken out in company. One reason the great instruments are great may be not only that they have been constantly played ever since they were made, but that they have been *well* played. They have, in a word, been taught to sing beautifully by the skilled players who used them. Every player must try to teach his instrument to sing. Careful tuning may well help this, since the A (or B, or C, or whatever) that the cello plays today will be the same as the one it played yesterday and will play tomorrow.

Perhaps I am too fussy about that A. But about the other aspect of tuning there can be no argument. The strings *must* be an accurate fifth apart. If not, notes played on open strings may be out of tune. More important, the player will have to adjust constantly the position of his left hand in order to play in tune. What his left hand learns one day, it will have to unlearn the next. Also, when the strings are an accurate fifth apart, a note played on one string will often cause other strings to resonate. This gives a richer tone, and helps the player know whether or not he has hit his note squarely. In short, when my cello is in tune, I can tell better whether or not *I* am in tune.

But to tune accurately is not easy for the beginner, even one with a fairly good ear. For one thing, the sound of the tuning fork has a different quality or color than the sound of the cello's A string, which makes it hard to match the string to the fork. For another thing, it is not easy, even for people with fairly good ears, to hear accurate fifths. Again, the fact that the strings have different tone qualities makes it hard to get them an exact fifth apart. Expert string players have learned to hear that fifth so accurately that they can tune two strings a fifth apart by playing them both at once. The ordinary player, and above all the beginner, cannot do that; his ear is not sharp enough. Indeed I once heard one of the world's great conductors say that he had just started to play the violin because his child was getting Suzuki training, and had found to his great surprise that even his beginning work on the violin had sharpened his ear.

But such thoughts did not lead to my inventions; the inventions came first, the thoughts later. What happened was this. One day, very early in my playing, as I was tuning up, the thought came to me that if the A string were exactly in tune with the tuning fork, when I sounded the fork and touched it to the bridge (the wooden piece which raises the strings up off the instrument), it ought to make the A string vibrate, and go on vibrating even when I took the fork away. I tried it. It worked. Then I began to wonder if it would work if the A string were not quite in tune. Soon I found that if the A string were *exactly* in tune with the fork, touching the vibrating fork to the bridge would cause the A string to make quite a strong sound. If the string were just a little out of tune, it would sound, but less strongly. If it were a little more out of tune, it would not sound at all. In other words, a tiny adjustment in the pitch of the string, a fraction of a turn of the fine tuning screw, would make a very noticeable difference in the loudness of the string's response to the fork. Knowing this, I could match the string to the fork far more accurately than I could with my unaided ear.

Beginning the Cello

I still had to decide whether the string was too high or too low. When the pitch of the string was very close to the fork, I could just as easily imagine that it was too high as that it was too low. There seemed no way to find the right spot except by trial and error. Many years later I made a discovery that helped solve this problem. I had already found that when there was a lot of background noise I could hear the fork and string more clearly if I pressed my ear against the tuning peg of the G string. One day, instead of touching the fork to the bridge and quickly taking it away, I left it touching the bridge, so that fork and string were sounding together. To my surprise, I heard a slow beat frequency, a slow rising and falling in the volume of the sound. By changing the tuning of the A string, I could make this beat frequency faster or slower (as piano tuners do). I soon found something even more surprising. If the string was a little sharper or higher than the fork, and I sounded them both together, I heard the beat frequency; if the string was a little flatter or lower than the fork, I did not. Knowing this, I could tell whether the string was too high or too low. Later I found that this beat frequency does not work on all cellos, and on some days does not work on mine. I can't explain any of this, but it is so.

For some weeks or months I tuned the A string to the fork in this way. But I still had the problem of tuning the D string a fifth below the A string, the F a fifth below the D, the C a fifth below the G. For this, I just used my ear and did the best I could. From somewhere I had learned that when two notes are a fifth apart, the ratio of their frequencies is three to two. (For an octave, the ratio is two to one.) It occurred to me one day that if two strings were an accurate fifth apart it might be possible, by sounding one with the bow, to make the other vibrate sympathetically. I tried it. Again, it worked. Soon I found exactly what I had found with the A string and the fork.

Inventions
165

A very slight change in the frequency of one string would cause the other string, a fifth away, to respond much more loudly or softly. Here, then, was an accurate way to tune all the strings. First I tuned the A to the fork, as described. Then I would bow the D string, then hold the bow on the string, stopping the sound. If the D was a fifth below the A, the A would sound sympathetically. By making slight changes in the D, I could make the A string respond more loudly or softly, until I found the spot that gave the loudest response. Then I would bow the G string, hold the bow on the string, and listen to the D. By pressing my finger on the G string at the very top of the string, right where it comes out of the peg box, I could make the G string a tiny bit higher. If this made the D string respond more loudly, I knew the G string was too low. Later I found that I could do this in reverse, that is, sound the D string and listen to the response of the G. When raising, very slightly, the pitch of either string causes the other to respond less strongly, then they are in tune. With the same process, I could tune the C. I have to do this quite often while I play. The cello (mine, at least) is very responsive to changes in temperature and humidity, and to the warmth of the player's body. In any practice session it takes a long while for it to settle into tune.

There are other tricks of tuning, well known to musicians, involving harmonics of the strings, or beat frequencies, which I won't take time to describe here. The really expert player may have no need or use for the tricks I have described. For the beginner, intermediate, or even advanced student player, it can be very useful. Years later I was invited by some students and teachers in the music department of a state university to talk to them about education. I said that I would prefer to talk about my adventures and discoveries on the cello. They agreed. One thing I talked about was this tuning invention. Some months later a friend, the conductor of the university symphony, wrote me that because of my talk the string players, all far more advanced than I was or will be for many years, were tuning more carefully, and had found that it noticeably improved their playing.

My other invention had to do with intervals, the musical distances from one note to another. I could not (still cannot) sight-read music, that is, look at a piece of written music and sing it. I do know enough to work out the tune, but only very slowly. I would be a better cellist if I could sight-read. But I have not yet taken the time to learn this, because, all things considered, it seems more useful for me to spend most of my music time at the cello itself. Still, even in the first year of my playing, I became interested in intervals, and felt it would be a good idea to learn them. At first I began in a more or less traditional solfège manner. That is, to learn the interval of a fourth, from *do* to *fa*, I would sing *do*-re-mi-*fa*, hear those two notes, sing them one right after the other, and try to remember them. But I couldn't remember from one day to the next the intervals I learned, and kept having to figure them out again. In time this might have worked anyway—many people do learn intervals by this method. But I wanted something better.

One day it occurred to me that I had a head full of tunes which must be full of all the intervals I wanted to learn. Why not get the intervals *from* the tunes? So I began, first with the smallest intervals, then gradually with the larger ones, to try to find pieces of music I knew well that used those intervals. Slowly I assembled my list. It is a curious mixture. Some of the intervals come from popular songs—the interval of a rising minor third comes from the first two notes of an old song, "Marchita" (perhaps "Marquita"). The falling minor third is the first two notes of the chant that children use to taunt each other. The interval of the fourth comes right out of jazz, the first two notes of the famous old Dixieland piece, "South Rampart Street Parade," which I learned at school from the wonderful Bob Crosby recording. For the sixth, I take the first two notes of the old NBC signature tune, or sometimes the first two notes of the old drinking song, "It's whisky (or beer, gin, etc.), it's whisky, it's whisky makes the world go round." But many intervals come from the classics. For the falling sixth I use the first two notes of the Second Chopin Piano Concerto, long one of my favorites. For the minor seventh I use two notes from *The Rite of Spring*, the same two notes of warning about which I write in talking about *Fantasia*. And so on. (See Appendix for my complete interval list.) The system worked. I should add, it worked for me because *I* matched the intervals to the music. Others wanting to try it would have to match their intervals with bits of their own store of remembered and loved music. For many people this trick might make the task of learning intervals much more easy and pleasant.

Giving Up the Alibi

While all this was going on, other parts of my life began to change. Pitman published my first book, *How Children Fail*. The Commonwealth School, where I had been coaching soccer and doing my practicing, asked me to teach some English classes for a couple of years, to fill in for two of their teachers who were taking sabbaticals. I liked the school and the students, had some ideas about teaching secondary school English that I was eager to try out, and needed the money, so I accepted. After a while, as *How Children Fail* became better known, groups of parents or teachers began to ask me to give lectures. And I was working on my second book, *How Children Learn*. With all this, I had less and less time for the cello. About this time Liz Titus's orchestra had to fold up; someone else took the room we were using, and even with much searching we could not find another place to play. The city was full of classrooms, unused in the evenings, which would have been fine for us, but no one would let us use them. So we had to stop.

The quartet, however, continued to play. We usually worked for an evening or two on a movement or two of a quartet, before going on to another piece. We were more interested in exploring a number of quartets than in trying to perfect any particular one. At the end of each session Liz would propose a movement or two of another quartet for the next meeting. Between meetings I would spend many hours studying my part, discussing it with Hal, working out fingerings and bowings, playing it with a metronome, almost memorizing it, so that when the time came to play with the others—always harder than playing alone—I could do so without making many mistakes. I was concerned about this; I felt very much (musically) the junior member of the quartet, and didn't want to hold the others back.

But as teaching and traveling and lecturing took more and more of my time, I had less and less time for practice. At the end of each quartet session I would promise myself to find a few hours to learn the piece we were going to do next time. But often the most I could manage was perhaps a half hour or so of warm-up and tune-up before we began to play, hardly enough even to look the piece over. I felt quite anxious and guilty about this. Even though I had been playing happily with these friends for more than a year, as I took out my music stand, music, cello, bow, and got ready to play, I could feel a small knot of fear in my stomach. Maybe I wouldn't be able to play any of the notes at all! Maybe I would wind up just sitting there! And so words of excuse would begin to form in my mind: "Listen, everyone, I'm afraid that I have to make a confession. I had meant to do some work on this piece, but I've been out of town almost all the time since we last met, and the fact is that I haven't even had a chance to look at it, so I hope you'll make allowances." I knew very well that if I did say something like that, the others would say, "Oh, that's all right,

John, don't worry about it, we'll understand, we'll take it nice and slow, or if worse comes to worst we can always play something easier." And so, with much patting on the head, and consolations, and reassurances, I could begin.

But I didn't say those words. I caught those apologies and excuses at the tip of my tongue and choked them back. They reminded me too much of too many children I had known in school. Fifth graders, even first graders, used to come up to me with their work saying, "I know it's wrong," or "I know it's no good." At first I used to reassure them, but in time I grew tired of this alibi-ing in advance. When they told me it was wrong, or no good, I began to say, "Well, if you know it's wrong, why not go back and fix it?" or "If you think it's no good, why show it to me?" Some of this I learned from Bill Hull. When children said things like this he used to say, very seriously and kindly, "What do you want me to do, pat you on the head?" The children would look surprised, for that was exactly what they wanted. But somehow, when he came right out flatfooted and *said* it, it didn't sound right. It made them feel cowardly, and though little children in school are often afraid, they don't like to be cowardly. Once in a great while, to Bill's question about a pat on the head, a child would answer or nod Yes. At that Bill, without saying a word, would reach out and very solemnly and ceremoniously pat the child two or three times on the head. After this ritual pat the child was usually ready to try to do whatever he had to do.

Remembering this, all in a split second, I would think to myself, "What is this anyway? Here you are, a forty-and-some-year-old man. Do you mean to say that you can't sit down and play a little music with some friends without first having to get a pat on the head like some timid six-year-old, just because you're afraid of making a few mistakes? *Either shut up and play, or go home!* But no alibis in advance, no appeals for sympathy. Do the best you can. If you can't play the music, let the others figure out what to do about it."

So I would say nothing, but sit down, tune up the cello, and in a spirit of "Well, here goes!," like a kid jumping off a high diving board, start to play. From this, I felt a great sense of release, freedom, and exhilaration. We are all afraid of many things; we probably can't help that. What we can try to do is not give in to our fears, but face them down instead. There is excitement in that. And with this small charge of adrenaline in me, I would plunge into the music. On the whole I did better than I thought I would. I made some mistakes, and lost my place now and then. But instead of giving in to panic, I tried to guess from what the others were playing when it was my turn to come in again. Much of the time I was right; they didn't have to stop for me very often. Only because I had to, I was learning some valuable skills of music that I had never learned before, how to guess and to bluff a little bit, how to get back on the musical wagon once I had fallen off.

After one such meeting, driving me back to the subway station at Harvard Square, Liz said to me, "You know, John, your playing has improved a lot." I said, "Oh, Liz, I never practice anymore, I can't do half what I could do a year ago, a lot of the time I'm just guessing and bluffing." She said, "I know that, but I'm not talking about that. What I mean is that you're really beginning to make music, to fit in with what we're playing, to sound like a real quartet player." I was surprised and pleased to hear this. I had thought I was only barely getting by; apparently I was doing better than that, and learning something valuable as well. So even without practice I went on with the quartet, and enjoyed it, perhaps more than ever. But after a while it too broke up; one player moved away, another became too busy. I also became too busy. Once again, this time to my great regret, music making dropped almost completely out of my life.

Giving Up the Alibi

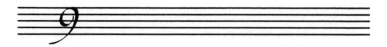

9

Intermezzo

My Work Crowds Out My Music

From 1966 to 1973 I spent most of my time away from Boston, working in different ways for educational reform. Many students, parents, teachers, teachers of teachers, and administrators asked me to come to their community to talk with them and others, or to visit and discuss the schools and classrooms which they were trying to start or change. These travels took me all over the United States and Canada, and also to Mexico, Great Britain, France, Germany, Denmark, Norway, and Sweden. When I was able to get home to Boston I was busy answering my heavy mail, or starting a small group of consultants to help teachers and schools to change, or writing three more books. This left no time for music making. I still went to Boston Symphony concerts when I could. At home, when busy washing, or shaving, or cooking, or eating, I continued to listen to records. But my cello, which my uncle Randall Davey had left me when he died, sat most of the time untouched in the corner. Now and then I thought to myself, "When the schools are what they should be, kindly, nonthreatening, interesting, and exciting places for children, it will be nice to start playing the cello again." That time, however, seemed many years away. Meanwhile the work seemed more important. Compared to it, playing the cello, making music, seemed no more than a hobby—an interesting hobby, but still only a hobby. Even as I worked, however, I still felt the pull of music.

Rehearsals in Indianapolis

When I was invited in the winter of 1969 to be a guest on a TV program in Indianapolis, I thought I would look up Izler Solomon, the conductor of the Symphony there. Years before, when he was conducting in Aspen, I had known him very slightly, and had liked his way of making music. I called him up, and he very kindly invited me to stay at his house and to go to an orchestra concert. We became good friends, and I found I admired his work more than ever. The Indianapolis Symphony was not as big and, player for player, not as good an orchestra as the Boston Symphony, but they played with a sensitivity and commitment that, in those days (but not these), the Boston Symphony did not always show. When my travels took me near Indianapolis, I began stopping by, whenever I could, for a visit with Izler, and a rehearsal or two and a concert.

These were some of the great musical listening experiences of my life. I have heard most of the world's great living conductors in person, and have watched quite a few of them rehearse the Boston Symphony. Among them Solomon seemed to me in the very top rank. Over the years I heard him and his orchestra give magnificent performances of many great works. Some of these performances, including a Beethoven Ninth, a Tchaikowsky Fifth, a Brahms Fourth, and Bloch's *Schelomo* (with the orchestra's principal cellist, Shirley Tabachnik) were the finest I have ever heard. Solomon was not only a fine interpreter of music, but an extremely efficient rehearser. His way of rehearsing was simple, at least to describe. He played long stretches of music at a time, whole movements wherever possible, stopped very seldom, and talked very little. Once, after a rehearsal, I said to him, half as compliment and half as question, "I can't get over how little you *say* to the orchestra during a rehearsal." In a quiet, patient tone of voice, as of one explaining the obvious, he said, "I can't talk to them during a concert." Exactly. Since the conductor can't talk to the players during a concert, he must learn to give information to them, and teach them to get information from him, without words. Of course, everyone who talks or writes about conducting *says* this. But even among the world's great conductors, not many do it. The gestures they use are often meaningless to the players —symphony musicians themselves have often told me this. Even those conductors whose beat is quite clear and expressive seem to think that if they want to change the way the orchestra is playing, they have to stop and tell them. Some of them, but by no means all, say what they have to say (as von Karajan wisely advised all young conductors) with simple word pairs like loud/soft, fast/slow, early/late, and so on. But almost all think they have to use words. Solomon rarely spoke. Once in a while I used to hear him say to the orchestra, as they played, "Dynamics!" meaning, "Pay attention to the dynamic markings (loud, soft, etc.) in your parts." He might use words now and then to correct mistakes or clear up confusion. But most of what he wanted to tell the orchestra about interpretation, he told them with gesture. He said to me once, "Because I don't talk to them much, they have to listen to each other," and I could hear that in their playing.

Another thing I learned from his work, useful not just for conductors, but for chamber music coaches and individual players as well, is that to learn to play a whole piece of music, one has to play the *whole piece*. Of course, like any musician, in learning a piece I have to take a bit at a time, and spend much extra time on the hardest bits. But at some point, if I am going to play the piece with other people, or in a perform-ance, I have to stop working on the bits and begin to play it as a whole—in musicians' words, have to "run it." Many con-ductors and coaches seem not to know this. They spend all their time polishing and perfecting this or that bit, hoping or assuming that at the performance all the bits will as if by miracle fall together into a finished whole. One veteran player in another major symphony said to me once, "For ten years it's been the same story; the first time we ever get a chance to play a piece through is at the concert." Small wonder performances of that orchestra so often lacked cohesion, flow, structure, tension. By contrast, almost everything I heard played by the Indianapolis Symphony came across as a *whole*, the first note connected to the last. They sounded that way because they had been rehearsed that way.

This is all the more important for beginning amateurs like me, of course, because it is so hard for us to learn to keep going. There is all the difference in the world between starting to play a piece thinking, "If we make a mistake or get in trouble, we can always stop and fix it up," and starting to play it thinking, "No matter what happens, we have to keep going." I wrote in the first chapter about the string quartet I now play in. When we began to "run" our lovely Mozart K.157, we found that not only did we grow more tense as we went along, but that when we made mistakes, we tended to keep thinking *back* to them, trying to correct them in our minds, thinking about what we should have done instead of what we were going to do. Our coach said to us, "What you have to do is keep thinking *ahead*, always getting ready for the next difficult thing that will be coming up." But it is only as we played the whole piece that we were able to learn to do this, to see further and further down the musical road ahead, to feel our playing as a journey through musical space and time.

The difference is a bit like this. Let us say you are driving for the first time to the house of friends. They have given you good directions, all the proper turning points, landmarks to tell you when you are coming to a turning point, landmarks to tell you that you made the correct turn. You arrive at the house without having made any wrong turns, without even having had any serious doubts or worries. But this trip will not be or feel at all like the trip you will make when you have been there ten or twenty times. Then, instead of having to follow directions, you will *know the way*. You will drive with a relaxed awareness of the landscape which is very different from the rather tense concentration with which you made the first trip.

Once I heard three successive rehearsals of the same work, Bartók's *Music for Strings, Percussion, and Celesta,* which neither Solomon nor the orchestra had ever done before. The first run-through was ragged, tentative, shapeless. It hardly seemed possible that they could get it ready in time for the performance. But each time they played it, they did it better. It was fascinating, and astonishing, to hear that beautiful and difficult piece come together, take shape before my eyes—or ears. For Solomon was still not doing much stopping or talking. He and the orchestra would run through a large section of a movement, he would stop, perhaps say a few words, and then they would do it again. Just by playing the music, the orchestra learned to play it better. Solomon knew that he did not have to *teach* them everything they had to learn; helped by his beat, they could learn most of it for themselves. And this was better, for what they learned for themselves they were less likely to forget in the heat of the performance.

Of course, these were pros, in a major symphony orchestra. They did not have to be shown how to play; the trick was to make them or rather *let* them play as well as they knew how to play. (A musician's compliment to a conductor is, "He lets us play.") A friend of mine once watched Solomon rehearse a student orchestra in a program that was much too hard for them. Here there was no use playing the piece over and over, they simply didn't know the notes, often could not even read their parts. For hours, with great patience and good humor, often a measure at a time (like Mr. Landers), he had to teach them, even sing them, what the actual notes were. He could do that, if he had to. But he preferred to let his players go as far as they could on their own. It is a lesson many conductors and coaches could stand to learn.

Another thing I learned from him, very helpful in my own work, is that given certain musicians and certain music you can only expect to get so much improvement in a day of practice or rehearsal. Aim for much more than that, and you may well get much less.

I try to put this understanding to work in my own practice. Quite often I am struggling to get a passage up to the proper tempo. I play it with the metronome, gradually increasing the speed, and trying to coax and trick my nerves and muscles into going faster than they think they can go. At some point progress stops. Sometimes I struggle on for a while, to see if I can control my tension. But I have learned to say to myself, after a bit of this struggle, "Okay, that's enough of this for tonight, time to try something else." In short, I am learning not to be too greedy for improvement. After all, even a tiny improvement in each day's practice will add up to a big improvement over a few months. Progress comes a step at a time, and it is wiser to be content with small steps.

All this I learned, without knowing I was learning it, from the work of this great and too little-known musician. For this, and other insights into music, and many great pleasures, I will always be grateful.

Rehearsals in Indianapolis

Meeting Janos Starker

During those years, whenever my travels took me near the Pacific Northwest, I used to visit my friends Eleanor and Henry Siegl, in Seattle. Eleanor, whom I had met first when she came to Boston, founded and still directs the Little School of Seattle, one of the most lively and humane elementary schools I have seen. Henry was and is the concertmaster of the Seattle Symphony. Often during these visits I went to orchestra rehearsals and concerts. Knowing my love of the cello, they invited me once to visit when Janos Starker, one of the world's greatest cellists, most of whose records I owned, would be playing the Haydn D-major Concerto with the orchestra. When I arrived, they had an extra treat in store for me. Starker had some very good friends in Seattle, and on one of the evenings he was to be in town they had planned a very small party for him. The Siegls were invited, and as their guest I was asked to come along.

It was a most interesting and delightful evening. Starker is an extremely articulate, witty, and intelligent man, and given the chance in the middle of a busy concert season to spend an evening with a small group of old friends, he relaxed and talked about many things, while the rest of us listened, delighted, making just enough comments or asking just enough questions to keep him going. I can no longer remember all he talked about. Much of it was about music and musicians, very perceptive, often very funny. Some of it was about a bridge he had invented for stringed instruments, and how he had come to invent it. I hung on his words, asked him a few questions about his bridge, and perhaps a few other things. I could not have enjoyed his company more.

Too soon the evening ended. Two evenings later I heard him play the concerto at the orchestra's concert—as usual with him, a brilliant, flawless performance. After the concert there was a party for the guest soloist and the conductor, at the home of one of the orchestra's trustees. The Siegls and I were invited. When we arrived, many people were there, but not Starker. I went over to the bar, got a ginger ale, and was standing there when Starker came in. Many people came up to be introduced to him. For a moment I thought of going over and saying how much I had enjoyed his playing. Then I thought this might be presuming on a very short acquaintance. Beyond that, I thought, what he probably wants is to have a drink and go home, not stand around talking. So I turned away; a moment later I heard a voice at my shoulder say, "Good evening, Mr. Holt." It was he. I said good evening, and added, as I was glad to, how much I had enjoyed his playing. He acknowledged this; then to my surprise he said, "Henry tells me that you play the cello." I made some sort of gesture, to suggest the enormous distance between my playing and his. Then I said, "Well, I started to play a few years ago, and worked hard at it for a couple of years, and loved it. Then I got involved in traveling and lecturing, and have more or less given it up. But someday I mean to take it up again, and to learn to play it well."

At this he looked at me long and thoughtfully. Then he said one of the most perceptive and truly helpful and encouraging things that anyone has ever said to me. He did not say, "I'm sure you'll do very well," or any such conventionally polite remark. It was not his style, and would have been neither true nor helpful. What he said, very seriously, was this: "Well, it's extremely difficult for someone of our age to learn to play this instrument well, because we have to develop a whole new set of muscles, and a whole new set of coordinations." He paused an instant to let that sink in. "On the other hand," he said, "we have an advantage." "What's that?" I asked. He said, "We can think up problems, and find solutions."

Think up problems! And find solutions! The Quakers have an expression, "He spoke to my condition." With those words,

Meeting Janos Starker

179

Janos Starker spoke to my condition. Perhaps something in my attentiveness to him two nights before, my great interest in what he was saying, the kinds of questions I asked him from time to time, suggested to him that I might take unusual pleasure in thinking up problems and finding solutions. Or perhaps he was just speaking of adults in general. In any event, nothing that he could have said could have done me more good. With these words he strengthened my hunch, hope, and faith, that old dogs *can* learn new tricks. Not only that, but can perhaps learn them even *better* than young dogs—once they get over the notion that they can't learn them. Which is what too many people—some of them music teachers—keep telling them. I thought about his words many times in the next days, weeks, months. The more I thought about them, the more I grew certain that if I wanted to make the needed effort, I could become a skilled cellist. Not on his level, no. But good enough to play, in chamber groups or orchestras, much of the great music that has been written for that lovely instrument. My inner voice said, if you want to do it, you can do it. As time went by I saw more and more clearly that I did want to do it, and would make whatever changes in my life I needed in order to do it.

The Fellowship of Music

Two other events made me want even more to get back into music. The first was hearing Peter Pears and Benjamin Britten perform in Jordan Hall, Pears singing, Britten accompanying him on the piano. In my exploration of music, I have never listened or felt much urge to listen to *lieder* or art songs. But I could not miss the chance to hear these two great musicians, who had worked together for most of their musical lives, on what would surely be their last visit to Boston. The concert was a moving experience. As ignorant as I was of that form of music (the form that interests me least), I could still hear and feel the extraordinary expressiveness and subtlety that these rare and great musicians put into their work. Even more, I felt how strong was their *partnership*, how deeply they understood and agreed on the music they were performing, and how well they knew, respected, and loved each other as human beings and musicians. Before doing each new piece they would glance at each other. In that short look were volumes of words—recollections, perhaps, of the many times they had performed that piece together, and even of the creation of the work itself, for much of the music they gave us that night was music that Britten had written for Pears to sing. Almost more than their talent, I envied them their friendship. I have long forgotten every note of the music they performed. But I will never forget what they showed me about what it can mean for people to make music *together*.

The other event that helped to push me back into making music was getting to know Apple Hill—to use its full name, The Center For Chamber Music at Apple Hill. One day Michael Steinberg, then music critic of *The Boston Globe*, invited me to have lunch with him and to meet someone he thought I would like to know. This turned out to be Gene Rosov, a young musician and very accomplished cellist, more or less the founder and for many years the director of Apple Hill. Knowing my great love of music, Michael guessed or hoped that I would be interested in Apple Hill and would want to take part in its work in whatever ways I could. He was right. I liked everything I heard about the organization, visited it, heard some of its concerts, joined its board of trustees, and, when I began to play the cello again, went there a number of times as student-musician-camper—of which more later.

Apple Hill, as its full name suggests, is a center for the playing, teaching, and performing of chamber music. It is what might be called a musical collective or commune, a fellowship of teaching and performing musicians. The place itself is an old farm, in Nelson, New Hampshire, near Keene. Quite a few of the fifteen or so young musicians who make up Apple Hill live on the farm, and more probably will as more housing becomes available. From June to September the farm, or the Center, is used as a music camp. There are four camp sessions, three of ten days each for musicians of all ages, from quite young children to people in their sixties or older, and one of five weeks for young players, mostly in their teens. At these sessions the student-musician-campers are divided up according to ability into performing groups, usually of three to five players, sometimes more. Each group is assigned music to play, usually one or two movements of a piece, and meets once a day for an hour and a half to work intensively on that music under a professional coach—one of the Apple Hill players. During the summer, and even more during the rest of the year, these same players give concerts in many places in southern New England, in Boston, New York, and other cities, and more recently even as far away as Florida.

It was at their Boston or Cambridge concerts that I first got to know some of these musicians. Strictly speaking, it was after the concerts, when they all went out to a local restaurant to eat, drink a few beers, and relax. Both in the concerts and afterwards I felt among them something of the same kind of understanding and friendship that I had felt from Peter Pears and Benjamin Britten. Not to say, of course, that in the world of music, even of Apple Hill, there is not some discord, jealousy, rivalry. But on the whole I felt very strongly that musicians who love the music they make are drawn more closely together by that work than most people are by either their work or their pleasures. The world of music, even at an amateur level, is a fellowship of a kind we don't see much of in modern society, and the more I saw of it, the more I wanted to be part of it.

My Music Becomes My Work

One day in the fall of 1969 Jonathan Kozol called me up to say that someone named Ivan Illich, whom I probably had not heard of (I had in fact seen one newspaper story about him), was going to invite me to teach some sort of seminar in Cuernavaca, Mexico. He said, "I know you are busy, but no matter how busy you are, you have to go, it's important." Not long after, Illich did call and invite me, and, remembering Jonathan's words, I agreed to go. I spent two weeks there the following winter, and each year thereafter for four or five years. These visits were for me very interesting and important. And though in Cuernavaca I never discussed music, except perhaps very casually in personal conversations, my work there had much to do with bringing music back into my life. The best way I know to describe what really happened at CIDOC in Cuernavaca is to quote the Nathan Detroit song from *Guys and Dolls:*

> It's the oldest established
> Permanent floating
> Crap game in New York.

CIDOC was a kind of established permanent floating seminar. It began with a discussion of schools and education. Illich himself was a very traditionally schooled man. As a result of his life and work in Puerto Rico and other poor Latin American countries, he had come to feel that, useful though they might be in rich countries, schools and schooling were a disaster for poor countries, and could only lock them deeper into poverty, ignorance, dependency, and helplessness. From this beginning he began to be interested in the whole question of educational reform in rich countries. He invited a number of people who had spoken or written, in the U.S. or elsewhere, to come to

My Music Becomes My Work

183

Cuernavaca. In theory, they were there to teach seminars. A more important reason for their being there was that Illich wanted to pick their brains—and wanted them to pick his. It was a thing often spoken of, but which too seldom happens, a meeting of minds. We were there to put our heads together, and all of us including Illich were much changed by doing it. In time we came to see that what was most wrong with modern people and modern societies spread much wider, and went much deeper, than schools.

The trouble and the problem was that people had become what Illich called institutionalized. That means, they had come to believe that anything and everything they or anyone wanted or needed, or might ever want or need, could be supplied and could only be supplied by some large, complicated, expensive, run-from-the-top organization. They saw every conceivable human good as the output of some sort of factorylike process. You want toothpaste? Design a factory and a process to turn out toothpaste. You want learning? Design a factory and a process to turn out learning. Call the process education, the factories schools or universities. You want health? Design a process to turn out health—call it medicine—and factories to carry on the process—call them clinics and hospitals. You want happy marriages? mental health? better sex? greater mobility? peace of mind? kind parents? successful children? Whatever you want, it is possible to invent a process and build a factory for turning it out; all that is needed are money, time, experts, and organization.

Institutionalized people turn human activities into commodities. What people used to *do* in order to meet their felt needs, now become things that people try to *get*. They turn verbs into nouns, like the words "learning" or "housing." To most people, "learning" is not the *activity* of finding out about this or that, something that anyone can do, but a product obtained from and in schools. "Housing" is not the *activity* of building or repairing one's dwelling, but a product obtained from the housing industry. "Health" is no longer the *activity* of living and working in a moderate and sensible way, but something which is "delivered." Society becomes a huge vending machine. Politics becomes arguments about what prizes we should put in the machines, and how we should distribute the tokens to get the prizes. People are told more and more that they are not even competent to decide what they need; experts will test them, or their children, tell them in what ways they have been found wanting, and prescribe this or that institutionalized product—drugs, therapy, training—to cure them, bring them up to snuff. This summary is too short to do justice to these ideas. Those who wish may explore them further in Illich's books—*Deschooling Society; Tools for Conviviality; Energy and Equity; Medical Nemesis* (in some countries, *The Limits to Medicine*). More and more people—Paul Goodman, E.F. Schumacher, Karl Hess, and many others—wrote or are writing about ways in which people, by themselves, with families and friends, in their towns and neighborhoods, can act directly and cooperatively to get what they need, instead of trying to persuade large, remote, uncontrollable, and increasingly unworkable institutions to meet these needs for them. This work of deinstitutionalizing people and society now seems to me perhaps the most fundamental and important political task of our times.

I did not go to Mexico to find an excuse or reason to play the cello. But these ideas, that grew out of my work there, became the bridge on which music making came back into my life. If I could learn to play the cello well, as I thought I could, I could show by my own example that we all have greater powers than we think; that whatever we want to learn or learn to do, we probably can learn; that our lives and our possibilities are not determined and fixed by what happened to us when we were little, or by what experts say we can or cannot do. In my work with the cello I might also find out things about learning music that might help many other adults learn it, or whatever else they wanted to learn. To many people, music now seems an unapproachable mystery. I hoped to find ways to make it something that all who wanted might take part in for themselves. In short, my love for music now seemed more and more joined to my love of teaching and to my deepest political concerns. The gap I had felt between my work and my hobby had disappeared.

10

Playing and Learning

The Beginner over His Head

In music as in tennis the beginner needs other people to play with. It's best if they play about as well as he does, or even a little better. Most of the time amateur musicians playing with others manage to do this—almost all the small groups I have played in have been quite well matched. But every once in a while I make a mistake, which can cause some embarrassment.

In 1973, not long after I began to play the cello again, I went to a New Year's Eve party with friends. At dinner someone asked us all to tell our New Year's resolutions. I said that mine was to start working hard on the cello again. Another guest, whom I had not known before, said, "Good for you!" and asked me what music I planned to work on. Among other pieces, I named the Brahms E-minor Sonata (for cello and piano). He said he knew the piano part, and suggested that we might play it some time. I said, "I'd love to, but I never played it very well and haven't even looked at it for years. Give me some time to work on it, and when I think I have it more or less in my fingers, I'll call you and we'll make a date." He agreed.

So I went to work. Except for a dab now and then at one of the movements of the Bach suites, or an exercise or two for variety's sake, for the next two months I spent almost all my music time, several hours a day (except when I was on a lecture trip), working on the Brahms. Years before, I had worked with Hal Sproul on the first two movements, and had glanced at the third, just enough to work out some fingerings. I had played the first movement once or twice with a student at the Commonwealth School, slowly and clumsily, with much stopping to get ourselves together again. But we had never even looked at the other two movements. Now I found to my surprise when I began to play the music again that much of it had stayed in my mind, so that most of the time I knew what it sounded or ought to sound like, and could tell when I made a mistake. But if my inner ear knew the piece, my fingers did not; they had to learn it again almost from scratch. Day after day, with great pleasure and excitement, I worked on it. Find the notes; figure out the best fingerings; learn how to play them more or less in tune; work out the rhythm—as in all Brahms, a bit tricky; play it with the metronome, at first at very slow speed, then slowly speeding up as I got the notes more and more in my fingers.

Besides learning my own part, I now had to learn how the piano part went and how our two parts fit together. I bought a recording of the piece, and listened to it over and over again, following with my eyes the notes on the piano score. I could not *read* those notes at all, but like a child who has the same favorite story read aloud to him night after night, after a while when I looked at the printed music I could hear the piano in my mind. (Could this be a way of learning to read music?) I tried to learn my own part so well that I could play it from the cello line in the piano score, without the markings and fingerings I was used to. As I played, looking at the piano part right under mine, I tried to hear in my mind what the piano would be playing at the same time. When I could do this fairly well, I went back to my own separate cello part and played from it, still trying to hear in mind what the piano would be playing. Much of the time I did this with the metronome, very slowly. Then, little by little, or as the Italian (and musical) saying goes, *poco a poco*, I would speed up the tempo. Or, I would set the metronome at a speed even quicker than the recording, read the notes in my part, and try to hear the music inside my head, or even hum it aloud. Again, I would see how fast I could do this, so that when I played the music at proper speed my mind, at least, would not think it was fast, having gone so much faster.

For two months the Brahms E-minor Sonata filled my mind. Day and night I heard it inside my head, as I did my other work, walked about the streets, traveled to lecture dates. Though I enjoyed lecturing, I hated to travel away from Boston, leaving cello and music behind, could hardly wait to get back to them. By the end of February I thought I was ready. I called up the pianist, and we made a date for the middle of March. Came the evening, I went to his apartment. In his living room was a fine baby grand piano. After a few words of greeting, we got ready to play, tuned, and began. The piece begins with the cello playing the main theme, mostly alone, the piano only putting in a note here and there. Then, as the cello goes on to another tune (or theme), the piano repeats the theme the cello just played. I began at what seemed a safe tempo, which must in fact have been much too slow. The piano came in, just as I had been hearing it in my mind for a month. I was nervous, but much more excited than nervous. Soon the piano had its tune to play. In the small room it made a huge sound; bowing inexpertly and timidly, I could hardly hear myself. I played ahead anyway. In spite of my nervousness, I didn't get lost, was able to keep going; we didn't have to stop very often. I know now what I didn't realize then, that this was not because I was playing so well but because the pianist was so good that he could stay with me no matter what I did. Anyway, on we went, finished the first movement, played the second, went on to the third, which I took at an absurdly slow tempo—it is supposed to be energetic and stirring, but I must have made it more like the galumphing of elephants in a mud wallow. Finally, the end. I stopped, sweating all over, exhilarated, amazed and pleased that I had been able to get through the music as well as I did. I said to my partner that this was the first time I had even played with anyone else in seven or eight years. He congratulated me warmly. Then we had a snack and a drink and talked about music for a while before I packed up and went home, my feet barely touching the ground. I thought to myself as I walked, "You played the piece! You actually played the piece!" I began to make big plans. We would play the Brahms again, I would work up one or more of the Bach sonatas for cello and piano—oh, we would do all sorts of stuff.

A week or so later I called again to see about playing some more, talked about doing the Brahms, perhaps another piece as well. Very politely he said, "I'm sorry, I'm not going to be able to play with you anymore." Down came my balloon to earth with a bump! I could hardly believe my ears. I managed to say how much I had enjoyed playing the Brahms, thanked him for working with me, and hung up. I was in a turmoil of feelings: surprise, confusion, disappointment, more than a little hurt. When I left his place, it seemed as if we had had a pleasant evening of music making together. What had happened? It could only be that he had decided that I wasn't a good enough player. Had it really been as bad as all that? For a while I struggled with these feelings of pain, shame, rejection, resentment—all the usual human stuff. After a while I began to see it from his point of view. Recalling our playing, I realized that not once had he made a mistake, not once had we had to stop because of anything *he* did. I began to understand that he was a really expert pianist, something close to a professional, perhaps studying to be a professional. Our playing together could not, musically at least, have been much fun for him, however well we might have liked each other. At my very first notes on the cello—timid, colorless, probably not altogether in tune, he must have thought, "Oh, my goodness, this guy really *is* a beginner, what have I let myself in for?" He had been a very good sport about it, and with his skillful and supportive playing had made the evening a great pleasure for me. But it was nothing he wanted to do again, and small wonder. I couldn't possibly blame him for that.

Looking back, I think to myself, a little in self-defense, "I *told* him I wasn't much good." But people never believe that. The trouble is, many amateurs say that they are much worse than they really are, to be "modest," to have their alibi in advance, to protect themselves against disappointment, and for the fun of hearing people say later, "But you're much better than you said you were." So amateurs tend to assume that most other amateurs are much better than they say they are. When I speak the literal truth, say that I am not a good player, or that I cannot play quick movements up to tempo, at least not without long practice, or that I am a very slow and uncertain sight reader, they say, "Oh, you're just being modest, I'm sure you'll do just fine." Sometimes I do "just fine." Sometimes I don't do "just fine" at all.

Once a friend invited me to some other friends' house for dinner and a musical evening. I said that I wasn't a good player. As always I was told that that didn't make any difference. At the house, the company was pleasant and the food delicious. Soon we began our music making. My first group played a movement or two of an early Mozart quartet. That I could manage all right. Then other people played, most of them much better than I was. After two or three more groups had

The Beginner over His Head

191

had their turn, someone said, "I know what let's do, since we have two cellists here, let's play the Brahms Sextet." A chorus of "Oh, yes, that would be wonderful, that's a beautiful piece, let's do that." The group began to form. Two of the players had years before graduated from music conservatories; two others were now attending one. I, who in five or ten years, if all went well, *might* become good enough to *enter* a conservatory, began to say that I had never even seen or heard the piece, let alone played it, and that I knew I could not sight-read Brahms. Everyone said, "Oh, come on, John, it's not hard, you can manage it, it will improve your reading, etc."

There seemed no choice, so I got my cello and took my place in the circle. Someone handed out the parts. At first glance it didn't look too bad; there were no forests of sixteenth notes, no long passages in the treble clef, no weird keys. I thought, "Maybe I can do it." It was not to be. We started off, and in almost no time at all I was lost. The notes looked fairly simple, quarter and eighth notes, but many of them were tied together, often across bar lines. By myself, studying the music, I can figure out that kind of rhythm quite quickly, but I can't do it, play, and count all at the same time. Once I lost the count, there was nothing in the music to help me pick it up again, none of the insistent rhythms, or harmonies, or cadences that in Haydn or Mozart might have helped me find my place. I stopped playing, thinking that if I did play I would almost surely be wrong, and would spoil the music for the others. But I kept trying to follow the printed music, looking for a place where I might join them again. After a while the others began to notice that I had stopped playing. Every so often one of them, trying to be helpful, would call out, "Eighty!" or the number of whatever measure they were playing. It didn't help; by the time I found the measure, they were somewhere else. A good musician, and not in a panic as by then I was, could probably have counted "two, three, four, eighty-one, two,

Playing and Learning

three, four, eighty-two, two, three, four, eighty-three . . ." and so kept his place until he found the right measure. That was far beyond me. I sat there, feeling a bit of a fool, thinking, "Why did I get into this?" still looking at the notes, hoping to find some resting place where I might come in again. There was none, and I spent the rest of the movement looking like someone who was just about to start playing, but somehow never does. After a while the others stopped calling out measure numbers to me, and went on with their now quintet. As we neared the end I thought about what to say or do next. I decided that if anyone spoke about my not playing, I would explain my problems in a few words and apologize for not having been able to keep up, but that if nobody else said anything, I wouldn't either. *Nobody did.* We packed up our instruments, other people played, the evening went pleasantly on. Were people being tactful? I don't think so; there was none of the strain in the air that there is when people are all thinking thoughts they dare not say. It just wasn't that important. Once again I realized, and said to myself as I have many times since and probably will many times again, "People are not all that worried about your musical problems and troubles, they have musical problems enough of their own. Play if you can, don't play if you can't, but in any case, shut up."

When at the start of this year (1977) I began to think of joining the Little Orchestra of Cambridge, I thought I would check in advance to see whether I would be in over my head again. On the phone I asked one of the leaders of the orchestra what sort of music they would be playing. He replied that I sounded as if I was a little insecure about my playing. I said, "I'm not the least bit insecure, I'm just not very good." But it sounded all right, I joined up, and it was all right. After a lot of practice, on the harder pieces I could get perhaps half the notes, on the easier pieces almost all of them. But one night during the summer what I had feared might one day happen,

The Beginner over His Head

did happen. *I was the only cello there.* Worse yet, we were going to read Bach's Suite no. 2 for Flute and Strings, which I didn't know. With a good player next to me, I could probably have played most of the notes; if I lost my place, I could quickly pick it up from her (all our good cellists were women). But by myself, I was lost. The music was just hard enough so that in thinking about notes and fingerings I would lose the count, and when I did, as in the Brahms, there was nothing to help me find it again. That I had once played that music, but on the flute, made things worse; I kept thinking the flute part instead of my own. A few of the movements were easy enough so that I could play them, but not the quick ones. At intermission, I wasted no time, but packed up cello, stand, and music, and left. I said nothing to anyone, no one said anything to me, or has since. No harm was done. I know now, I can get in over my head, but I won't drown, not in music.

On Being Hard on Myself

There are other crippling and self-destructive thoughts that I am trying, and slowly learning, to chase out of my mind. Our piano trio decided one day, before we went to work on the Mendelssohn, to warm up by reading some Haydn trios. In all of these the piano and violin parts are much harder than the cello part. But my pianist and violinist friends are both very good readers, and while they were playing their parts very nicely, I was having trouble with mine. I began to feel not only frustrated but embarrassed, even a little ashamed and guilty. A voice in my mind began to say, "What's the matter with you? There's nothing in your part but quarter and eighth notes, you ought at least be able to play *them* right." Of course, these thoughts only made me play worse. After a short while I took hold of myself, and began to say to that scolding voice in my mind, "Shut up; what difference does it make what they can do, or what I *ought* to be able to do? I am doing the best I can, and that is all I can do." After silencing that scolding voice, I said to my playing self, "Don't worry, do your best, you'll get better."

These same thoughts tend to sneak up on me when I am playing in the Little Orchestra. Among the pieces we have worked on this year (1977) are the first four of Dvořák's *Slavonic Dances*, several movements of Brahms's First Serenade, and Beethoven's Second Symphony, all lovely music, and all harder than almost anything I have played. Sometimes it takes me many hours of practice to figure out the notes and learn how they should sound, still more time to figure out the best fingerings and bowings, and still more to get the music into my fingers. Then I start playing against a metronome, slowly increasing the speed as I get the feel of the music. With much hard work I manage to increase my speed fifty or even a hundred percent. Then I listen to a recording of the music and find to my dismay that the speed I have reached with such effort is still only half the correct speed. At orchestra rehearsal I see the four cellists in front of me rattling off this music at the proper tempo, even the first time they have seen it. The inside voice begins to say, *"They* can play it; why can't *you* play it? What's the matter with you? What makes you think you are *ever* going to be able to play this instrument?" The other day I was practicing a passage, nothing very quick or complicated, mostly quarter or eighth notes. But I was having trouble getting my fingers to play it. Once again the voice began to tell me that the music was easy and that I *ought* to be able to play it. Once again I had to remind myself that "ought" has nothing to do with it; if it was hard for me, then it was hard, that was all there was to it.

Every now and then I find to my surprise that I am threatened, made resentful and anxious, by the greater skill of others.

On Being Hard on Myself

195

Oddly enough, I am much less threatened by the enormous skill of the players in the Boston Symphony than I am by the lesser skill (but still much greater than mine) of the cellists in my own little orchestra, or the players in some of our local amateur or youth orchestras. The great soloists, like Starker and Rostropovich, and the Boston Symphony players, are so far beyond me that I don't even think, much less worry, about being that good. But I sometimes feel discouraged when I think how much I will have to improve just to be as good as the other players in my orchestra. To have to work so hard to get not into the major leagues, but just the lowest of the minors! But then I realize that this business of comparing myself with others, or berating myself because (so far) I can't do what they can do so easily, is silly. The baby learning to walk does not reproach himself every time he falls down. If he did, he would never learn to walk. When he falls down he gets right up and starts to walk again. Just the other day I saw a little girl at this stage; she was walking like someone on a ship in a very rough sea. In the hour or so I was near her she must have sat or fallen down thirty or forty times. Up she rose each time and went on her way. Not being able to do what she was trying to do may have been a nuisance, but not *failure*, nothing of which to feel guilty and ashamed.

What I am slowly learning to do in my work with music is revive some of the resilient spirit of the exploring and learning baby. I have to accept at each moment, as a fact of life, my present skill or lack of skill, and do the best I can, without blaming myself for not being able to do better. I have to be aware of my mistakes and shortcomings without being ashamed of them. I have to keep in view the distant goal, without worrying about how far away it is or reproaching myself for not being already there. This is very hard for most adults. It is the main reason why we old dogs so often do find it so hard to learn new tricks, whether sports or languages or crafts or music. But if as we work on our skills we work on this weakness in ourselves, we can slowly get better at both.

Learning Process

One reason I am a better learner of music now than when I began to play the flute is that I understand better what has to happen and does happen in my mind, nerves, and muscles when I learn. This process is not linear, not something that I can divide into step 1, step 2, step 3, etc., each to be done before I do the next. What I have to do is build, or better yet grow, and as I grow fit together a number of different but related structures in my mind, nerves, and muscles.

When a raw beginner looks at a piece of music, he sees groups of five lines and on them arrangements of little round dots and other marks. What they mean, what they would sound like, how to make them on the cello, he hasn't the faintest idea. The skilled cellist, looking at the same notes, knows: 1) The names of the notes, A, C, D, F-sharp, etc., 2) what key these notes are in, 3) if these notes make some sort of chord, what chord that is, 4) the musical intervals between the notes, that this note and that note are a third apart, or a fifth, etc., 5) the rhythmic pattern that these notes make, 6) what those notes should sound like, 7) where those notes are on the fingerboard of the cello—and they are all in more than one place, 8) the various motions of fingers, hands, arms, and bow—and there are many of these, some easier or more musical than others—that would produce those notes. He has built all of this knowledge so completely into his mental-muscular model that as he looks at these notes his ears hear them and his arms, hands, and fingers play them.

Each one of these eight pieces of knowledge is not a list of separate items, but a structure, more like a map, or a three-dimensional model. The eight maps or models are not all the same, but they are all related and fit together, just as maps of the U.S., showing contour, temperature, rainfall, geology, population, etc., give different information but are all about the same reality.

These are the structures that I have to grow and at the same time fit together in my mind.

Knowing this helps me in my work with the cello. Many adults, learning to play an instrument, think of their learning process as a long series of little steps. Their teachers may even encourage them to think this way, perhaps hoping that looking at one step at a time will seem simpler, easier, and less discouraging than seeing the task as a whole. Instead, it is often much more discouraging. Adults who see their learning task as a long series of little steps are very likely to think of their own playing and practice as a long series of little tests, each with one right answer and a great many wrong ones. Every time they try to play something, they are taking a test; if they don't play it right they write an F or zero in their mental grade book. In time these failing grades mount up, and they get discouraged and quit.

For if Right means playing it the way Starker or Rostropovich or Rose or Yo-Yo Ma would play it, *everything* we do is wrong.

But we don't and never did learn complicated skills by dividing them up into a series of tiny steps, each of which we had to get right before we could go on to the next. Some like to say that we have to learn to walk before we can learn to run. Not so; babies start trying to run while they are still very clumsy and uncertain at walking. The growing baby advances into the world on a great many fronts, doing as many things as he can, none of them very well, but all of them a little bit better each time. It is the same for the novice advancing into the world of music.

Playing and Learning

It is like learning to whistle, which most of us did, without being taught, when we were little. We did not learn by learning to whistle one note perfectly, then another note perfectly, and so on. We learned to whistle tunes by what mathematicians call successive approximations, trying a number of times, never getting it quite right, but getting a little better each time.

This process never ends. There is a lovely story about the great cellist Pablo Casals. When he was in his seventies, not quite the player he had once been, but still very good, a friend came to visit him in Puerto Rico. Casals, as he always did, began the day with a walk along the beach, his friend with him. Then back home, to play a little Bach before breakfast. Casals took out his cello, tuned it up, and began to play a C-major scale—the C, on the open string; then the D, with his index finger; then the E, with his third finger. Here he seemed to get stuck. He played the E, played it again, went back to the C, the E again, then the open G string, back to the E, and so on. The friend looked on amazed. Could Pablo Casals, one of the world's greatest musicians, be having all this trouble with a simple C major scale? Casals struggled on, and after a while looked up, saw his friend staring at him, and wise old man that he was, read his thoughts, "Always," he said, "every day for fifty years, I have to find the E."

Yes. Every day, we have to find the E. It is not a matter of finding it, once and for all, when we begin to play, and then having it forever. We have to keep finding it.

This leads me to the second important point about the process of learning to play the cello. Most of it is not verbal. That is, it is not a matter of knowing a list of rules which, if you can only make yourself follow them, will cause you to make good music. Take for example the very basic problem of changing the direction of your bow with the least possible interruption of the sound. When the beginner does this, the sound stops, then starts again, often with an audible squeak or scratch. With the expert, one can barely hear those changes of bow. But this does not mean that there is some rule or rules which the expert can tell the beginner to enable him to make a smooth, *legato* (that is, unbroken) sound when he changes the direction of his bow. That isn't what happens.

To understand what actually does happen, we can draw on some of the thinking of the behavior modifiers and operant conditioners. Most of their ideas seem to me at best trivial, at worst sinister. But in this matter of bowing, they really do seem to give a clearer picture of reality. When I practice, like all string players I spend quite a bit of time trying to make smooth changes of bow. I try to imitate the way good players move their hand and arm, and to feel what my own hand and arm feel like when I do. I bow back and forth, back and forth, and as I bow I listen. Some of my changes of bow will be smoother than others, some even quite good. When I hear a good one, I don't stop and ask myself, "What rule did I follow that time that I didn't follow the other times?" I couldn't answer such a question, and even if I could, it wouldn't help me. Instead, I keep on bowing. My ear tells me, "That last bow change was nice; whatever you did then, do it again," and that is in fact what happens. I don't know what I did better, in the sense of being able to *say* it, but knowing that it was better, my nerves and muscles try to do the same thing again. This whole process, this cycle of feedback, reinforcement, and correction, completely bypasses the part of the mind that asks questions, gives answers, makes and follows rules. I don't *need* to know, in the sense of being able to *say*, what I did to make a smoother bow change. As long as I pay attention to what I am doing and hearing, whatever I did well, I will tend to do again.

The same is true of getting a good sound out of the instrument. I get a much more even and warmer sound out of my cello than I used to. But this is not because I am now following some rule that I wasn't following then. There are no rules for getting a good sound from a stringed instrument. There is nothing that we can *tell* a novice that will enable him, then and there, to make a nice sound. We can say a few rules about bowing: don't dig the bow into the string, but on the other hand, don't let it skate over the string; try to keep an even pressure and an even speed; make sure the bow doesn't slide up and down the string as you bow. But one can do all these things, and still not make a very nice sound. The thing to do is to bow, and as you bow, to listen. When you hear a note that is nicer than most of your notes, think "Aha!"—and keep bowing. You may not know what your muscles did that was different, but whatever it was, they will tend to do more of it.

What all this boils down to is a kind of law of learning that I have finally come to understand and accept:

WHEN YOU'RE WORKING, YOU'RE LEARNING.

When I was teaching school, a man came to a parents' meeting and complained about the extraordinary amount of testing we were doing. His words went right to the heart of the matter: "You're like a gardener who constantly pulls his plants up by the roots to see if they're growing." That is just what we were doing, and what I have finally learned not to do to myself.

We don't have to ask ourselves every day, "What have I learned, am I learning anything? Am I learning enough?" If we're working, doing our best, challenging ourselves, doing things that are hard for us, and sometimes very hard, paying attention to what we hear in our ears and feel in our muscles, not letting our minds wander or think about something else— if we are fully involved in our music making, interested in it, excited by it, then we are learning. We may not and probably cannot know all of what we are learning. We are almost certainly learning much more than we think. By our work and our attention we are helping to grow the musical structures I spoke of earlier. If we are patient, we will find, as I am constantly surprised to find, that we *know* more than we consciously

Learning Process

learned, even things that we never set out to learn. A friend of mine who played the piano quite well when young and then after many years took it up again in middle-age, put it perfectly: "It's amazing, I can feel my hands growing *intelligent,* they know how to do things that I didn't tell them."

There is nothing mysterious or magical about this. The point about structures of knowledge is that they are much greater than the sum of their parts. We can put on one piece of paper a map of a city. From that map we can find an infinite number of ways to get from any point in the city to any other point. If we tried to write down all those possible journeys, one by one, we could fill a warehouse with them—and still have less information than we could get from the map. In the same way, as we build into our minds, nerves, and muscles these musical maps I have spoken of, we are using a finite amount of information, of *conscious* learning and practicing, to build structures that will generate an almost infinite amount of information, and what is more important, do it almost without conscious thought. This is, after all, what we're aiming for: to get to the point where we have only to look at the music on the page, or perhaps only hear it in our mind, for our intelligent hands, without having to be told how, to make the music for us.

This can create a paradox, a tension. At times we must think very hard with our conscious, planning, questioning, critical mind. At other times we must tell that part of our mind to shut up. Timothy Galwey has written very well about this in *The Inner Game of Tennis,* a very good book for all students of music—for music is, after all, and in more ways than one, a kind of athletics. It involves and requires not just muscular strength, quickness, and effort, but also the ability to be aware of many things at once, and above all, the ability to keep cool and do one's best under pressure. Galwey's central point is that after we have taught our body to do something, we must then learn to get out of its way, leave it alone, and let it do it. Once our hands have become intelligent, we have to trust their intelligence, not keep butting in asking, "Are you sure?"

This has been very difficult for me. I think of an example. It is harder for cellists than for violinists and violists (and harder still for bass players) to hit high notes accurately. In the first place, the left hand has to move further to hit the notes. In the second place, where in high positions the left hand of the violinist/violist is to some extent anchored and positioned by the instrument itself, the left hand of the bassist/cellist is floating in the air, has nothing to guide it. We must rely entirely on the feeling of the muscles themselves to hit the notes squarely. A friend of mine, an expert cellist, once showed me an exercise to help me hit those notes, and build a better map of that part of the fingerboard into my nervous system. In this exercise I close my eyes and play a note, say C, in a low register, to get the sound of it in my ear. Then, eyes still closed, I let my left hand hang at my side, trying to see in my mind's eye and to feel in my muscles where I will have to put that hand on the fingerboard to get a C in the highest or next to highest octave. Then, eyes still closed, I bring up the left arm, put my finger down on what I hope will be the proper spot, and play the note. If I miss, I make the proper correction, try to get the feel of that spot in my muscles, and then try again, until I can hit that note several times in a row. Then I try other notes, and vary the exercise in other ways.

It is a spooky exercise. Closing the eyes makes it much harder; when we play notes in the high positions, even though there are no marks on the fingerboard, we get more cues from our eyes than we think. And with eyes closed I feel a touch of the uneasiness that all people who ordinarily see feel when suddenly they can't. When I tried this exercise for the first time, it seemed impossible, and I missed the notes by wide margins. But I was astonished at how quickly I improved; quite often it only took one or two corrections before I was able to hit the target, even several times in a row. At first, not much of this skill transfers from one day to the next; the second time I tried the exercise, I was hardly any better at it than the first. But gradually the muscles and joints of shoulder, arm, elbow begin to "know" where those notes are. Someone once wrote that in addition to the traditional five senses, we should add a sixth, our skeletal awareness, our ability to tell the angles that our limbs and trunk make with each other. It is this sense that "tells" the left arm and hand where to go.

The exercise is spooky in still another way. When I set out, eyes closed, to hit a certain note high up on the A string, I feel uncertain, slightly anxious; I don't think I *can* hit it. What is surprising is that I feel just as uncertain and anxious even after I *do* hit it. It seems only blind luck, not something I can expect to do again. About a year ago, as I write, I was working with a clarinetist on the first two movements of the lovely Brahms Clarinet Trio in A minor. At one point in the slow movement the cellist plays a short phrase that drops down to the lowest D on the instrument. The next note, only an instant later, is a high F-sharp, about three and a half octaves up, almost the entire range of the instrument. Going for that note I felt the way I felt as a kid when I climbed to the top of the high diving board and jumped off. It seemed a great leap out into nothing. The clarinetist and I worked hard on that section, and in time I could hit that F-sharp on the nose about three times out of four. But I never *expected* to hit it, and therefore always played it more timidly than I should. The trouble is, cello playing *still* seems to me something of a miracle.

It is partly because I have not yet learned to trust my hands to do what I have taught them to do that I am still a very slow sight reader. Faster than I used to be, and faster all the time, but still too slow. Part of my problem when I read a new piece of music is that I meet groups of notes that my hands don't know how to play. I am not yet familiar enough with these patterns of notes to be able to react to them without thinking. I have to think consciously about the intervals and the fingering. But the other part of my problem is that even when my hands are playing notes that they really do know how to play, the thinking, criticizing, worrying part of my mind wants to keep butting in, saying, "Are you sure that was right? Are you sure that was right?" instead of doing what it ought to be doing, which is looking ahead to see what the hands are going to have to do next. I can hardly believe I am right, even when I am. Like the anxious child in school, looking for a reassuring pat on the head, I want to hear a Big Voice in the Sky saying as I play, "That's right, John, that's right, you're doing fine, go ahead, keep up the good work." As with so many other things, knowing that I have this bad mental habit does not mean that I can cure it right away. But the more I understand what I am doing wrong, and why I do it, and why I ought not to, the sooner I can learn to stop doing it. And the most harmful habits we are likely to have in trying to learn music are not strictly physical habits, putting this hand here when it ought to go there, but mental and emotional habits, ways of thinking and feeling about ourselves and the problems and failures we meet in our work.

When I began the cello, and was taking lessons from Hal Sproul, I learned from my exercise book (Piatti) that my left hand could be in either the open or closed position. In the closed position there is a musical interval of a semitone between each of the four fingers; in the open position there is a whole tone between the first and second finger. The student also learns another meaning of the word "position," to describe how far up or down the fingerboard his left hand is. Reading on, I found that whether my left hand was in open or closed position would depend on: 1) What key I was playing in, 2) whether the key was major or minor, 3) which string I was playing on, and 4) what numbered position, up or down the keyboard, my left hand was in. Thinking of all these variables, I began to panic. All that to memorize! Like a good student in school, I began to make up a kind of table to help me do the memorizing. I told Hal about this. He laughed and said, "Oh, you don't have to bother with that." I said, "But don't I have to know all that to know how to put my hand on the fingerboard?" He said, "Yes, in a way you'll have to know it, but that isn't *how* you'll know it or *how* you'll learn it." He was right; as I built up my musical mental structures, my hand simply went to the correct notes. Of course, if I now have to play a piece in a key with many flats or sharps, I first have to play some scales in that key to "teach" my hand where to go on the fingerboard. When I first tried to play a piece in the key of E (four sharps), I began by *thinking* in the key of C, and trying to remember each time I had to make a note sharp. This was very hard, as hard as it would be for me now to try to play atonal music. After struggling with this for a while I thought, maybe this would be easier if I learned to play the scale in the key of E—and it proved to be so. Soon the hand knew where to go.

So, knowing that whatever is interesting and challenging helps me to grow these musical structures, I don't have to torment myself with questions about what I ought to do next, or whether I am learning the right things, or anything at all. When I am interested, energetic, alert, and attentive, then I am learning. I try to play a wide variety of music and exercises, work on many different pieces at once, do some things that are much too hard for me, just for the fun of trying them out. Most of my exercises come right out of the music I am trying to play. Quite often these difficult bits tell me that I ought to put in some extra time on a certain exercise. In a piece I am working on right now there is a passage in which I have to bow across several strings. Since at first I didn't play it very well, I thought it might be wise to spend some time doing the arpeggios (which go across all the strings) in Feuillard (my exercise book). I did, and enjoyed it very much. Last night, as I write this, I spent an hour or two struggling with some very difficult double-stopping exercises (meaning playing on two strings at the same time) in Feuillard. I don't need them for anything I am playing, or am likely to play for some time. But every few months I like to take a shot at them, because they are so hard, and so different from anything else I do. And I was pleased to find that last night I could play them much better than the previous time I worked on them. This is what is so wonderful about music. There is so much to do, such a large number of interesting exercises to work on, so much beautiful music to read, learn, and play with others. I have no problem with boredom, or not knowing what to do next. My only problem—which I may never solve—is finding enough time to do all the things I would like to do.

Some Teachers

I learned quite early how lucky I was to have Hal Sproul for a teacher. One day I arrived at his house a few minutes early. Through an open living room window I could hear someone playing the Prelude to the First Bach Cello Suite, which I was also working on. Through the window I could see that it was another student, a young man. Curious, I listened for a while. His intonation was probably a little better than mine, his tone only fair. He was playing the right notes, and in time. But it sounded like a machine playing. Every note was exactly like every other, there were no accents, no ritards, there was no variation in the dynamics, no flexibility in the rhythm, no shape to the phrases, no color, no poetry, no feeling. I had never heard playing like that; how could one be that accurate, and yet play with so little expression?

In a few minutes, when my lesson time came around, I rang the doorbell. Hal called to come in. In the living room the other student was packing up his cello. Hal introduced us, we said hello, and the other student left. As I was getting ready to play I asked, "Who is that?" Hal said it was someone who had just started to study with him. After a moment or two, he asked, "How long do you think he has been studying the cello?" I said I didn't know, probably a little longer than I had. Hal told me he'd been studying seven years. I said, "Seven years! Who's he been studying with?" He named one of the world's great cellists, an internationally known concert player, professor of cello at a hotshot music school, and so on. I said, "What in the world has he had this guy doing?" Hal said, "Playing exercises." Poor devil, he had had his seven years of drudgery, and still hadn't begun to have any fun with his cello.

One evening a woman about my age joined our little cello section in Liz's orchestra. The two good players being in front, this woman and I shared the second cello stand. She played about the way I did, only more timidly. Of course, she may have been a little reticent, playing in a new orchestra. At break time, as players always do, we began to talk about our music. She asked how long I had been studying, and with whom. I said with Hal Sproul, for a little over a year, and asked her the same question. She said she had been studying for five years, with someone who had once played in the Boston Symphony. I then said "What music does he have you working on?" She said, "Oh, he doesn't let me play any music." I said, "Doesn't let you play any *music?* Then what do you play?" She said, "Exercises." After a second or two she added, "Every so often he says to me, 'Perhaps I will let you play a little Vivaldi.' But then after a minute or two he says, 'No, no, you are not ready yet.'"

Once again I thought how lucky I was to have the teacher I had. I thought also of what Sam Piel had told me about his teacher in New York, a very old but (among cellists) famous teacher. Sam had asked him one day what exercises he should play. His teacher said, "Exercises! Exercises! Why play exercises? Play *music!* When you find something hard in the music, learn to play it beautifully. Make that your exercise!" Much of the time I follow this advice. On the other hand, there are many exercises that I *like* to play. Sometimes I feel a real itch to play four-octave scales, or arpeggios, or thirds, or double stops; I can hardly wait to get to my Feuillard. But I play them not just because they are interesting and challenging, but because I know they will help me play more easily and beautifully whatever music I am working on.

Learning without Lessons

The trouble with most teachers of music or anything else, is that they have in the back of their minds an idea more or less like this: "Learning is and can only be the result of teaching. Anything important my students learn, they learn because I teach it to them." Teachers make this belief clear by the way they teach, or talk about their teaching, or react—usually with anger—to the suggestion that their students might find out for themselves, and be better for finding out, much of what they are being taught. It is not enough for them to be helpful and useful to their students; they need to feel that their students could not get along without them.

All my own work as teacher and learner has led me to believe quite the opposite, that teaching is a very strong medicine, which like all strong medicines can quickly and easily turn into a poison. At the right time (i.e., when the student has asked for it) and in very small doses, it can indeed help learning. But at the wrong times, or in too large doses, it will slow down learning or prevent it altogether. The right kind of teacher can be a great help to a learner, particularly of music. The wrong kind can be worse than none. In the four years or so since I began to play seriously again, I have been on the lookout for the right kind of teacher. One, whom I liked both musically and personally, and thought might be ideal, was and is far too busy to take on someone as unskilled as I am. Another, strongly recommended to me by a cellist friend whom I trust, is out of town most of the time and in any case is tired of teaching and wants to stop. Meanwhile I continue to learn a great deal on my own. What kind of teacher I want, and why I want that kind and not some other, is what this chapter is about.

When I began to play the cello, and took lessons from Hal Sproul, he was the perfect teacher for me. I loved working with him, and can hardly imagine how I could have gotten started without him or someone like him. When, at age fifty, I began to play again, I took three lessons from a cellist friend, then stopped. Though I have since played a good deal of chamber music under professional coaching, I have had no further individual lessons. This seems to shock many people. When they ask, "Who are you studying with?" and I say, "No one right now," they are surprised; some even become indignant or angry. Why am I *not* taking lessons, they demand to know. How do I expect to learn anything unless I do? The answer is that some of what students get from their teachers, I no longer need or can get in other ways, some I am not yet ready for, and some I don't want at all.

One of the main reasons many students take lessons is so that they will practice. Again and again you hear them say, "I have to go and practice. I have a lesson coming up, and my teacher will jump down my throat if I'm not prepared." I don't need any such goad or threat. I like to play four hours a day, more if I can. Travel, or the pressure of other work, often make this impossible, but if I don't get close to four hours of playing I always feel the day is a bit wasted. Also, teachers suggest to students exercises to work on and music to play. Beginners need this. Without Hal Sproul's suggestions, I would have had no idea how to begin. Had I known other cellists, I might have asked them, but I didn't know any. I had never heard of Bach's suites for cello or the Brahms E-minor Sonata, and even if I had, would probably never have thought of trying to play them, had Hal not suggested them. But now I know what music there is to play, enough for ten lifetimes, and if I need a particular kind of exercise, know ten people to ask. Time is my problem, not ignorance about what to play.

To the beginner the teacher also suggests ways to organize practice time. He says, Work fifteen minutes on this, five minutes on this, half an hour on this, and so takes from the students the burden of making such decisions. He gives a model of what good cello playing should look and sound like, against which the students can measure their own playing. He gives feedback and corrections about the students' playing that they themselves don't yet know enough to make. He solves technical problems for them, shows them how to finger and bow difficult passages. He suggests how they might interpret the music, i.e., says, Play louder here, softer there, lighter here, slower there. He makes judgments about the students' progress. And, if he is good, he inspires by his own example; the students are eager to practice not because they are afraid of the lesson but because they want to make music as beautiful as their teacher's.

All this help was valuable to me at the start. Now, for the most part, I no longer need it. Organizing my practice hours, and keeping enough variety in my practice, is a problem interesting in itself; I like to think about it, wouldn't want to turn it all over to someone else. From records, and from seeing and hearing many great cellists, I know what good cello playing looks and sounds like, what I want my own playing to look and sound like. I know enough about what I am doing wrong to have more than enough to work on. I prefer to try to work out

Learning without Lessons

211

my own bowing and fingering problems, before asking others for help. Playing a passage with many different fingerings is a good exercise in itself. Also, I am more likely to remember under pressure a fingering that I have worked out on my own, and from working on such problems I get criteria and problem-solving skills that help me with the next music I study. The more musical puzzles I figure out, the more I *can* figure out. And I don't need weekly judgments about my progress, either to scold or reward. The metronome, the tapes I sometimes make of my own playing (something quite a few professionals have told me they would never dare do), the music itself, tell me what sort of progress I am making, sometimes more than I had hoped or expected, sometimes less.

The time will come, or at least I hope it will, when I will need more feedback and advice about fine points of execution and interpretation than I can get by myself. The March 1977 issue of the *Johns Hopkins Magazine* has a very interesting article, by Robert Kanigel, called "The Making Of A Musician," in which he describes the work of Robert Pierce, principal horn of the Baltimore Symphony and Professor of Music at the Peabody Conservatory. Here he is working with one pupil:

> They run through a series of *études*. One calls for rapid hand-stopping, a technique for closing off the bell of the instrument with one's hand to deepen the sound. Another demands conformance to a tricky beat pattern in 9/16. Finally, they're set for Richard Strauss's *Ein Heldenleben*, a piece . . . that Marc is to play with the Peabody Symphony Orchestra.
>
> "It seems to me," says Pierce after one passage, "that those sixteenths are coming in too soon." Marc goes back and plays it again, this time to his teacher's satisfaction.

Kanigel writes later:

> But crucial as technique is, and elusive as is its mastery, you
> don't get picked for the Chicago Symphony because you can hit
> the right notes. That's where interpretation, or "musicianship"
> comes in. How to taper a phrase or stress a note. How to
> convey the nuances of feeling no musical notation can fully
> represent. How to breathe life into a score written for another
> time and place. . . . Week by week, the comments, suggestions,
> and interpretations leave their mark. Week by week, as if by
> osmosis, the teacher's musical standards are instilled in his stu-
> dent.

I would like nothing more, someday, than to be good enough
to work in this way with such a teacher. Without such teaching
I will probably never become the player I would like to be. But
that's not where I am right now. What I need most, right now,
is not someone to help me with interpretive problems. I know
much more about how I ought to play and want to play than
I can put into effect.

As I write these words, our Little Orchestra is getting ready
to play a couple of small free public concerts—in which we
usually outnumber the audience. One piece we will play is the
Finale—*vivace*—of Haydn's Symphony no. 101, *The Clock*. It
ought to go, and we will try to play it, at about half-note =
MM126. The movement has a number of eighth-note passages
for the cellos which at that tempo are much faster than I can
play. I have been working on them for weeks. Last night and
today I have spent several hours practicing them with a metronome, trying in many ways of my own invention to coax or trick
my nerves and muscles into playing them at the proper tempo.
The best I can do, so far, and then only after much practice,
is to get them up to MM88. At the concert, I will have to cheat
—play the first three notes in each group of four, and skip the

Learning without Lessons

fourth. I don't need an expert teacher or weekly lesson to tell me that I need to work on trills and many other kinds of speed exercises. Or, when I find it hard to read the simple cello part of a Haydn piano trio, I don't need to be told that I need to work on sight-reading. What I need is good advice about how to learn to play faster and read better. But I collect this advice all the time from experienced musicians I know.

I also read every book about cello playing I can get my hands on. *Cello Playing of Today,* by Maurice Eisenberg, himself a pupil of Casals (published by *The Strad* of London), is one of the best, in spite of a pleasantly nutty theory that vibrating one's hand in the air over an open string can change the sound of the note. There are many others, often with equally nutty theories. The books almost always say that there is only one right way to do this or that, and often disagree with each other about what the right way is. But I can usually find one or more interesting and valuable ideas in any of them. Between what I learn from musicians (which they may have learned from their teachers), and what I find in these books, and all the exercises and tricks I have invented myself, I could easily spend eight hours a day just working on speed and on sight-reading —and I have many other things to work on as well. Someday I hope to work with a cellist equivalent of Robert Pierce. To try to do it now would probably be a waste of my time and his (or hers).

There is another kind of teaching which I don't need or want, now or ever. One musician I know put it very well. "My students," he said proudly, "do exactly what I tell them, and only what I tell them, or they can't work with me." As a niece of mine used to say when very little, "No thank you for any." I am not somebody's lump of clay. Other teachers have a lifetime's supply of speeches about music all bottled up inside them, under high pressure. Every lesson gives them a chance to make some of the speeches. I'd be glad to hear these over a friendly beer, but not in a lesson at X dollars per hour. Still other teachers, like teachers of most sports, have elaborate theories about playing that they want to try out on their students. Expert cellists say to me, or someone, "When you play, be sure to do this or that." But when I watch these same cellists, sometimes with binoculars, in practice, rehearsal, or concert, to see whether they do what they tell their students to do, I find that quite often they do not. A cellist will tell me that there is only one way to do something, when I can see many of the world's great cellists doing it some other way. To be sure, in spite of small differences, the playing of all the great cellists has certain qualities in common, and it is those qualities that I am looking for. Some cello teachers like to say that in holding the cello bow this finger must be exactly here, that one exactly there. The truth is, as I have heard Janos Starker say, there are many good ways to hold a cello bow. What they all have in common is that the bow hand must be comfortable, unstrained, flexible and secure.

This matter of strain and tension is crucial. Almost all musicians and music teachers can and will tell you how important it is to relax. But many of them are themselves extremely tense. Like all anxious teachers, they pass their tension on to their pupils, even as they are telling them to relax. How many times have I heard people say, "I played terribly at my lesson, I was so nervous, couldn't do anything right." A good teacher, like Hal Sproul, helps his students *not* be nervous, helps them play *better* than they usually play, not worse.

A friend of mine, a fine amateur violinist I met at Apple Hill, has such a teacher. In Boston we spent a long and absorbing evening talking about his work with that teacher, and what the relationship between a serious student and a good teacher can be at its best. As when I saw Pears and Britten play together, I envied him. This friend, even though skillful, had always been a very tense player. Even his mental image of good violin playing was tense. His teacher not only told him to relax, which all teachers do, but told him *how,* showed him things to do which helped him to relax. I've tried them, working on music which is hard for me, and they help *me* to relax. That's the kind of help I am looking for.

I need help with hard problems of fingering and bowing in the music I am playing with others. Most of these problems I can work out for myself, but now and then one stumps me. When my three friends and I were working on the Mozart String Quartet K.157 there was one such passage which came twice in the first movement. It looked easy enough on paper, but I must have tried a dozen different ways to bow it, without ever finding one that was both comfortable and musical. A good teacher might have told me, "Well, there really isn't a good way to bow that, but this way is probably the least bad, so work on it." In a Beethoven duet which I am playing with a violist friend, there is a short passage for which I can't find a really good fingering. Everything I try feels awkward. A good teacher could probably say, "This fingering may feel awkward at first, but in time you'll find that it works." Most of these problems I would still try to work out myself, but if I spend a certain amount of time on one without finding any solution I like, I am ready for expert advice.

I need ideas—beyond those I have already—about ways to work on a number of specific weaknesses: sight-reading; counting while playing; trills; quickness in general; shifts up and down the string; changing both string and position in one shift; left-hand flexibility. I need more critical feedback, more criteria for judging my own playing, more things to pay attention to in practice. Again, I practice very attentively right now, but there still might be something important that I am overlooking. Most of all, I need the experience of playing for a critical listener, to get over any stage fright I might feel about that, and to learn to play my best under pressure—just as in sports. But even while giving me this help, the teacher I need must accept that he or she is my partner and helper and not my boss, that in this journey of musical exploration and adventure, I am the captain. Expert guides and pilots I can use, no doubt about it. But it is my expedition; I gain the most if it succeeds and lose the most if it fails, and I must remain in charge.

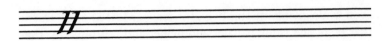

Apple Hill

A Musical Year

In the fall of 1973 I began to play seriously again, an hour or two a day at first, then, as my fingers became tougher and my hands stronger, often three or four hours. To make more time for playing, I decided not to make more than two lecture trips away from Boston in any week, or stay away from home more than two days at a time. All this time I had been going often to Apple Hill for meetings of the Board of Trustees. At some point I began to think of going there as a camper-student. It seemed a very bold idea at first. But Gene Rosov encouraged me, and in September I went to a five-day session. I played in two groups, one doing the first movement of the Mozart G-minor Piano Quartet, a dramatic and lovely piece, the other doing two movements of a Mozart flute quartet. I loved everything about the session, and planned to go again as soon as I could. One of the teachers had talked about my playing in a quartet in the Boston area that winter, but nothing came of it.

In any case, between writing my book, *Instead of Education*, and lecturing, I had much less time for music that year than I wanted. The next May I went to Apple Hill again, a great experience, of which more later. Since Apple Hill didn't seem to be turning up any people for me to play with in Boston, I decided to look around on my own. I got in touch with my old friend and coach Liz Titus, to see whether she could turn up something. She was glad to hear from me again, and by happy chance had a quartet that needed a cello. The other three and I got along well musically and otherwise, and met weekly at the Longy School in Cambridge, where along with some sight-reading we worked on Haydn's delightful Quartet op. 33 no. 6. Soon after, a clarinetist I had met at Apple Hill suggested we play some clarinet trios. We never did find a pianist to play with, but during the winter the two of us worked on the Beethoven Trio, the trio arrangement of the Beethoven Septet, and the first two movements of the very beautiful but very difficult Brahms Trio.

I went to Apple Hill again the following summer. In the fall our quartet started to meet at the New School of Music in Cambridge, where we worked first on two movements of Haydn's Op. 20 no. 6, then on Mozart's Quartet K.157. Meanwhile I joined a violinist and a pianist friend of hers in a piano trio, working mostly on the Mendelssohn D minor. Then in late January I began playing with the Little Orchestra of Cambridge. We worked for a while on two short contemporary works, plus the *Eight Russian Peasant Songs* by Liadov and a few of the Dvořák *Slavonic Dances,* which we performed at a couple of free concerts. Later we worked on two movements of Beethoven's Second Symphony and several movements of the First Brahms Serenade. Most of this music was too hard for me, at least at the proper tempi, but I grabbed what notes I could. All in all, it was musically a busy and productive year.

A Musical Year

The peak of it all was another visit to Apple Hill. Let me try to give the feel of the place by describing a typical day.

Music Round the Clock

I wake a little after 5:30 A.M. For a few minutes I enjoy my warm sleeping bag in the cool early morning. The woods outside the cabin are full of birdsong; I recognize thrushes, but no others. After a while I crawl out of my sleeping bag and push shut the sleeping-loft window beside me. I dress as quietly as I can and slip down the stairs to the floor of the small cabin. My four roommates are still asleep. I pull on my boots, collect music, music stand, and other gear, and get ready to leave. The lawyer, also an early riser, opens a good-morning eye at me. I wave a greeting and go outside. The woods are light, with an early morning greenish-grey light, but the sun is not yet up over the hill—no telling what kind of a day it will be. Up the steep hill and into the main building. I seem to be the first one up. The Winter Dining Room, the largest heated room in the camp, is full of instruments left there for the night. I pick my cello out from a bunch of cellos and violins, set up music stand and music, and begin my morning practice. Soon the sun comes over the top of the hill and lights the top of the trees on the hills rolling toward the west. After a while my lawyer roommate, an oboeist, comes in, greets me, lies down on the floor, and starts his morning back exercises. Then he takes out a little black box of tools and with a little grumbling begins his daily chore (bassoonists' also) of carving and shaping reeds. I play on. The sound of a radio playing rock music in the kitchen tells us that the cooks are up and starting to fix breakfast. It's not my day to be a waiter, so I don't go in to help them. Around eight o'clock other people begin to drift in and pick up their instruments. I pack up my cello and music and go in for breakfast, a quiet meal. My groups don't meet until after lunch, so after breakfast I loiter around for a while in the main room of the barn, listening to five very skilled players working on the Dvořák Piano Quintet. Then back to our cabin for more practice. On the way down the hill I stop by another cabin where two of my other roommates, a dentist-oboeist and a flutist, are working with a high-school clarinetist and two college students (French horn and bassoon) on the Nielsen Woodwind Quintet. For a few minutes I listen to the music, which I love, but I need to work, so I go on down to our cabin and play. After the first period, still another roommate, a college professor and violinist, comes in and lies down on his bunk for a nap. I go back up the hill to search for a place to practice. The mudroom of the farmhouse is occupied; so are the two small practice cabins halfway down the hill. Another cellist has found the old auto seat in the shop and is playing there. I go back to the main building and down to the laundry-furnace room, but my dentist-oboeist roommate has beaten me to it. I try my last resort, the dressing room next to the men's shower. It's not ideal, much too "live," the sound of the cello is almost deafening. But I get something done.

So until lunch. The big room of the barn fills up with people, talk, laughter, noise. Waiters bring food to the tables and we fall to. After lunch some announcements, usually followed by sardonic comments. Then a couple of groups perform for all of us the music they have been rehearsing. The wind quintet plays the Nielsen, a fine performance of a very difficult piece. Then I go down the hill to a cabin to meet with my Haydn group, of which more later. In the final period I go to another cabin to work on a trio with two other cellists. The period over, I join some others at the small soccer field in the woods. We choose up sides, both sexes and all ages, and soon a fierce game is going. Many of the resident musicians are soccer nuts (as I am), and get quite stern with me if I miss the daily game. We

Music Round the Clock

get very hot in the sun, and knock off in time for a swim in the pool before dinner. One of the campers, a middle-aged woman and a superb swimmer, is finishing her daily fifty or sixty laps. People gather on the lawn in front of the barn, waiting for dinner. I lie down on the grass, take a short nap. Dinner is ready, and so are we; music makes you hungry. After dinner more groups perform. The official day is over, the evening is ours, we can do what we want.

What most people want is to make more music. Some groups meet with their coach for an extra rehearsal. Most people get together in informal combinations, anything from duets to a small orchestra. I wander around, trying to find out if anything extra interesting will be going on. Some of the pros and a number of the best amateurs will be playing the Brahms Serenade no. 2 in the main barn at nine o'clock. Later some pros will be rehearsing a piano quartet they will soon play at a public concert. I make a note of both events; until then, I will practice in the cabin. Both my dentist and lawyer roommates are bustling around organizing evening groups. The dentist has the trunk of his car packed with music; when he wants to play something, he has parts for everyone, not just himself. I envy the evening free-lancers. I would like to do that, but am not a good enough player or sight reader. Someday, maybe. Meanwhile, I need all the practice time I can get for the pieces I am playing with my groups. I go back to the cabin and work on them.

Later, by the time the Brahms serenade is over and the pros have rehearsed their quartet, it is close to midnight and my bedtime. But some people are just getting going. The chief fanatic is a young violist, just out of college. Daytimes he works around the camp to earn part of his tuition for the coming five-week session. Evenings he free-lances. Since good violists are scarce, he keeps very busy. When not playing he rushes from room to room, wherever other players can be found, trying to organize something. His schedule is as complicated as an airline's. I hear him saying, "At one o'clock we're going to be doing the Beethoven in the farmhouse, but we should be through with that about 1:45, so why don't you meet us there then and we'll find a place where we can go to work on the Brahms." And so on until three or four in the morning. Next morning, when I come up, I'll be pretty sure to find him in his sleeping bag in a corner of some room, catching a couple of hours of sleep before his day begins. But I can't stay up like that anymore; I have to go to bed. As I go down the hill toward the cabin and sleep, I can hear behind me, very faintly, the sound of a piano in the barn.

A Haydn Quartet

A few weeks before the May 1975 camp session, Apple Hill sent me the cello parts to the music that my groups would be playing there. One piece was the first movement of Haydn's String Quartet op. 20 no. 5. The cello part looked disappointing; it seemed to be mostly repeated eighth notes, sometimes followed by a quarter note. Just da-da-da-da-da-da over and over again. I thought peevishly, "Why didn't they send me anything more challenging than this? Do they think I can't *play* anything harder than this?" I had no idea how hard that simple part would be to play.

That evening I put the music on the stand and began to work on it. Even by itself my cello part was harder than it looked. To begin with, it was in the key of F minor, four flats, a key I had never played in. And, as in all Haydn, there were places where the music moved into a number of keys. It took me a while to find the notes of my part, get used to what it sounded like, work out good fingerings, and learn to play it in tune. I bought a pocket score of the quartet (The Kalmus pocket score of the thirty *Celebrated Quartets*). From my recording of the Op. 20 Quartets (by the Tatrai Quartet) I made a cassette tape of no. 5, and played the first movement many times, looking first at my own part to see how it fitted into the music, then at the score to see what the other three players were doing. The movement is basically a somber and beautiful solo for the first violin, set in a powerfully rhythmic accompaniment by the other three instruments. It is deeply emotional music, and I soon began to love it and to look forward to playing it. When the time came to go to Apple Hill, I packed up rough clothes, camping gear, music stuff, and a small cassette recorder so that I could play my tape for the other members of the quartet. Riding up to Keene, New Hampshire, on the bus I played the movement over a number of times, following in the score, trying to reach the point where just by looking at the written notes (which I still could not read) I could hear in mind what the others would be playing.

At Apple Hill I said hello to all my friends, found my cabin, and settled into the familiar and happy routine of music camp life. On the schedule board I found the names of the other members of my groups and when and where we would be meeting. Our coach for the Haydn was Richard "Dobbs" Hartshorne, the resident bass player of the Apple Hill Chamber Players. We had worked together before and had become good friends. It being too cold for us to practice in one of the unheated cabins, we planned to meet in the bedroom of the tiny apartment in which he lived. At our first session I met the other members of the quartet. The first violinist was a high school senior; the second violinist was a high school sophomore or junior; the violist was a woman in her twenties who had been a good flutist and had recently switched to viola. We went to work. Right away I found out that the simplest-looking music is often the hardest to play. As the first violin began her solo, the other three of us played together a da-da-da-daa figure, three eighth notes followed by a quarter note. We spent much of our time in the first two sessions just working on that figure, trying to get our eighth notes the right weight and length, and all exactly the same.

Dobbs was a patient but very exacting coach. What he wanted from us was a performance as close to professional standards as we could get in a week. Except for the first violin, our parts were simple enough so that we could play the bare notes without too much trouble. Our problem and task was not technical, but artistic—to play those notes with all the awareness, concentration, sensitivity, and meaning that a great quartet would put into them. At first progress was slow. Like all unskilled musicians, we tended to play everything at one dynamic level—moderately loud. It was hard for us to dig in enough to play really strongly, harder yet to play really softly, hardest of all to do one right after the other. Yet the music often goes from very soft to very loud, or vice versa. And Dobbs wanted the louds *loud* and the softs *soft;* listening later to the Tatrai Quartet's recording of the music (which many critics consider the best), I realized with some surprise that their loud and soft were less contrasted than ours. Sometimes these dynamic changes came very suddenly, sometimes in long crescendos or decrescendos. It was hard for us all to get louder or softer at the same rate. It was harder yet (as it is even for good musicians) to play louder without playing faster, or softer without playing slower. Bit by bit we became at home in our own parts so that we could begin to hear the others and get the feel of the whole piece.

Two things I remember about our rehearsals. At one point the first and second violins have a rapid sixteenth-note figure which they toss back and forth to each other, while the viola and cello stick doggedly to their da-da-da-daa accompanying figure. The effect is of a battle, the high voices trying to overpower the low ones, the low ones fighting back. Yet the second violin comes in a sixteenth note earlier than the viola

A Haydn Quartet

and cello, so we had to be sure to hear her first note before we played ours. This may have made us too tentative. One day as we were playing that passage Dobbs said loudly—to me? to all of us?—"Insist!" I can still hear his voice saying it. It was just the right word. Later, in one place the music goes from loud to very soft, while at the same time the harmony makes a pronounced change. It is a hair-raising moment, and Dobbs wanted us, as we played our insistent rhythmic figure (which by now I almost heard in my sleep), to make just the slightest pause before that dynamic and harmonic change, not enough to slow down the music, more like a faint catch of the breath. In our excitement we would either forget to do it, or do it too much and so spoil the effect by calling attention to it. And we had to be sure, after that tiny pause, *not* to slow down the tempo.

By the last day of camp we had improved a lot, but had really never managed to give Dobbs more than a part of what he was asking for. The plan of the day was for all groups to meet in the morning for a final half-period rehearsal, and then perform their pieces before the whole camp in the afternoon. We met for the last time in the tiny bedroom, barely big enough to hold us. For a while we worked on spots, hard places. Near the end of the period Dobbs said, "Let's run it once." We began, and as if by a miracle everything began to come together. All the things he had been trying to get us to do, we did. As we realized that we were beginning to do it right, we stopped thinking and worrying and the music took over. We insisted where we should insist. The fortes were strong, the pianissimos just a breath. We came to the place for the tiny pause, and managed it just right; I could hear Dobbs say softly "All *right!*" On to the stirring coda and the dying-away end of the piece. We sat for a few seconds, all five of us too surprised and moved to speak. Then we slowly got up and began to pack our stuff. As we left, Dobbs said, "Whatever happens this afternoon, nothing can take that performance away from us."

After lunch the groups began to perform. The wait for our turn seemed endless. A couple of groups before our turn, I left the barn and went into the farmhouse for a last-time run through my part. After an age we took our places before the audience, set up our music, tuned. A signal from the first violin, and we began to play. For a moment I was too busy battling against stage fright, struggling to concentrate on the notes of my part, to hear the whole quartet. But I soon became aware that once again the music had taken over and that we were playing well. Only at one point, where the parts weave in and out of each other, did we get just a bit apart.

I still don't know whether it was my mistake or someone else's, and, if it was mine, what it was. The violist, who had had a lot of orchestra experience as flutist, saved us, or at any rate saved me. She said "G," just loud enough for us to hear, meaning, of course, rehearsal-letter G in our parts. I—we—picked up the place instantly. Luckily I was able *not* to brood about what went wrong, but to stay with the music. It was our only slip, and perhaps only Dobbs noticed it. From there to the end, pause and all, we played as well as we had that morning. Once again after the coda and the dying-away ending, we were so moved that we hardly dared look at each other; I felt that it would have taken no more than a touch to make me cry. I dimly heard applause. Somehow we got ourselves off the stage. Dobbs came up, as moved as we were, congratulated and thanked us, as we thanked him. The afternoon concert went on, ended; people packed up, said good-byes, went their ways. A jolly lady, a violinist, gave me a ride back to Boston. The session was over.

Only, in a way it wasn't. In the next two days I must have relived in my mind, twenty, thirty, fifty times, the experience of playing that quartet. I don't just mean that I heard the music again in my mind. I mean I *felt* myself playing the music, felt

A Haydn Quartet

227

again all the emotions I had felt while playing it. Only after a couple of days did I come fully back to Boston and the here and now. Slowly the experience and the music began to sink into unconscious memory. It is still there, still powerful. This morning, before starting to write this chapter, I played that tape again, looking at the score, and was again much moved. I wondered, as I have many times before, why music should have the power to move me so. "What's Hecuba to him, or he to Hecuba...." Millions, hundreds of millions of people suffer, starve, and die all over the world. Their pain worries, saddens, and angers me, but it does not make me weep. Why should music? I don't know. I'm not sure I want to know.

Haydn Again

In 1977 I signed up for the second ten-day session at Apple Hill, from the first to the eleventh of July. One of my two groups was to play the first movement of the Haydn Quartet op. 9 no. 1. The music looked challenging; there were some passages of sixteenth notes that I knew I would have to work hard on. I couldn't get a score, but fortunately the Aeolian Quartet in London had recently recorded the Op. 9 Quartets as part of their recording of all the Haydn quartets, so I was able to hear what our first movement sounded like. It was delightful, vigorous, good-humored music, Haydn at his hearty best.

At Apple Hill much had changed in a year. The old barn, which had been our main concert hall, dining hall, and central meeting place, had been much renovated and extended. The smaller barn had also been renovated, and new cabins had been built. We arrived on Friday evening and began work the next day. Our Haydn group met in one of the cabins first period after lunch. There I met the other members of the quartet, an even younger group than I had played with two years before. The first violinst was Heidi Willmann, thirteen; the second violinist, Debbie Miller, was a high school senior; and the violist was not quite thirteen. Our coach was Mowrey "Moby" Pearson, who often played first violin with the Apple Hill Chamber Players. We began work on our music. As in all Haydn quartets, the first violin part was hard. The three lower parts, particularly the viola and cello parts, were also somewhat more complicated than in Op. 20 No. 5, and in some places fit together in tricky ways. One very strange and modern passage, full of tritones, appeared twice. It was very hard to play in tune, since Haydn had in a way made it deliberately out of tune. And there were contrasts of loud and soft to look out for. Moby was a splendid coach, patient, understanding, demanding, with a very sure sense of how much he could ask for at any one time. As a violinist he could of course help the violinists and violist with their parts. One day he played each of their parts in turn, while the player sitting out acted as temporary coach, following the music in the score as we played and commenting about what she heard.

Day by day the piece came together. It was a good group to work with. We were all serious and attentive; we practiced our parts in between sessions and came prepared to work; we liked our coach and he liked us. Our morale was high. We had planned to play only the first movement, and perhaps the minuet, at the end of the session. But at the midpoint of the session I had an idea. Debbie, our second violin, who like Heidi was a fine player, had said that the music she had to play in her other groups was not much of a challenge. I suggested that in addition to the first movement of Op.9 No.1 we begin work on the slow movement, with Debbie taking the first violin part and Heidi playing second. We seemed to be working so well together that I thought we might be ready to perform both movements by the end of the session. Everyone liked the idea, and we decided to try it.

The slow movement of Op. 9 No. 1 is a quite plain but very beautiful solo for the first violin against a simple accompaniment by the other three strings. At least, our three parts looked simple—mostly quarter note plus eighth note, quarter note plus eighth note. They turned out not to be at all simple to play. We had to play those quarter and eighth notes exactly together and at exactly the same loudness or softness. No part could stand out, it had to sound like one instrument. At the same time we had to match our tempo, phrasing, and dynamics to the solo violin. Much of the time the whole point of our accompaniment was that the audience should hardly be aware of it. And as in Op. 20 No. 5, there were a number of sharp contrasts in dynamics. At the very end of the piece, right after a big crescendo, was a measure of piano, then the last two measures pianissimo. The piano had to be very soft, and the pianissimo noticeably softer yet. To make all this happen we had to work even harder than in the busy and energetic first movement. Every time we rehearsed, in spite of telling myself, "Relax! Relax!" I could feel the back of my neck and shoulders tighten up, less in nervousness than in concentration. After an hour's work on this movement, I would be wrung out—exhilarated but exhausted. It seemed a miracle that professional musicians could keep their concentration and emotional edge through a long and difficult program, without getting either too tense or too tired to play.

As we neared the end of the session I began to think about our coming performance. At such times in the past my mind had liked to run a delightful little home movie. The plot was simple. First I played my part perfectly, then everyone told me so. Experience had taught me that this movie was bad for me, and that when I caught myself running it I should quickly turn it off. Not that vanity is all bad; without some cockiness and conceit no one would ever have nerve enough to perform at all.

Apple Hill

But beyond a point vanity becomes a danger. To want success too much invites failure. The more I feel I absolutely *must* play well, the more I worry about making mistakes. The more I worry, the more mistakes I make, and the worse I am thrown off by any I do make. My home movie was bad for another, more subtle reason. I play the cello as often as I can before others to give myself practice playing before an audience, and to get over a state of mind which tends at such times to hinder and spoil my playing. It is not exactly "stage fright"; I feel it when I am not afraid, even when I am eager to play. But I find that I can't concentrate, can't focus my thoughts and energies on the music. It is as if my mind, my being, my *soul*, was somehow leaking out into the room. I am not *here*, inside my skin and inside the music, but out there. I play as if in a trance or a dream.

So when I get ready to play, I must not be thinking about *them*, the audience, or about what *they* are thinking, but about *it*, the music, what I and my colleagues are about to do. This time, much more than ever before, I was able to get into that frame of mind. I wanted our quartet to give a performance that would make the audience love the music as much as we did. I wanted us to play well not to get praise, but for our own pride and satisfaction, so that we and our coach might feel that all our hard work had accomplished something. My only fear was that by playing badly I might let down my colleagues, or perhaps that all of us, as amateurs often do, might give a careful, timid performance, correct enough but without energy or spirit.

Our final run-throughs went well, the best yet. We were to perform the first movement on Sunday evening, the slow movement the next day. After dinner, just before our turn came, Moby wisely had us tune together in another room, so that when we came onstage we could begin right away to play. We took our places, I announced what we would play, we

Haydn Again

looked at each other, Heidi gave us a signal, and we began. Any fears I might have had about this being a timid performance disappeared with the first notes. My three colleagues just sailed into that music, and I with them. Before we were halfway into it, my nervousness had disappeared. I began, in a way I never had before, to *enjoy* playing before all those people. I was not thinking, and my colleagues did not seem to be thinking, "Can we get through the piece?" No, we were thinking, and trying to express in our playing, "Hear this fine music of Haydn's. Isn't it lovely?" In that spirit we played quite a bit better (which had never happened to me before) than we had played in any rehearsal. As two years before, I was nearly overcome with the excitement of playing together, the beauty of the music, and pride and pleasure that we had played it as well as we had. For the first time I felt nothing at all of, "Whew! we got through it!" I would have been glad to sit down and play it again.

Next day, when we were to play the slow movement, I felt no nervousness whatever, for myself or the quartet. I knew that we had something lovely to play for the audience (which would include Heidi's parents), and I was eager to have us play it. Unlike the busy first movement, the slow movement begins softly, which is a harder way to begin. Strong playing can cover up some insecurity; in soft playing everything shows. But by the time we had played the first couple of bars I knew we would be all right. As we played, I felt, more than ever, that we were not just four amateur musicians who happened to be playing the same piece, but a real quartet. Within the limits of our skill, we were beginning to think and play like one person. So we played the movement, again, it seemed to me, quite a bit better than we ever had before, ending in a whisper. We stood up, much moved, took our bow, left the stage, slowly came down to earth. The concert ended, people slowly said their good-byes and left. By evening Apple Hill seemed deserted and silent.

Apple Hill

Moby and I and some other friends went out for dinner, then one of them drove me into Boston. As I had two years before, for the next two days I played over and over again in my mind those two lovely movements of Haydn, feeling once again all I had felt. Now, four months later, I feel many of those same feelings again.

Epilogue:
Clearing a Space

As I write this last chapter, it is mid-November, 1977. Our string quartet in Cambridge, with a new violist, is working on Mozart's String Quartet K.458, *The Hunt,* a lovely piece, but much harder than the K.157 we did last year. Two other friends and I have begun work on Beethoven's String Trio op.9 no.3, a very exciting piece. The violist in that trio and I are also working on Beethoven's *Eyeglasses* Duet. I have found another pianist—like the first, a much better musician than I am—willing to play the Brahms E-minor Sonata with me, so I am working on that again. The Little Orchestra of Cambridge has been rehearsing, and has played in one concert, Mozart's Sinfonia Concertante for Winds, Beethoven's *Leonore* Overture no.1 (very hard for us), and the finale of Haydn's Symphony no. 101, *The Clock.* We are now beginning to work on the rest of *The Clock,* Mozart's Overture to *Idomeneo,* and Bartók's *Roumanian Folk Dances.* I sight-read as much new music as I can, including the cello parts to all the late Mozart quartets. And there are all those exercises, interesting in themselves, to make my hands stronger, quicker, more flexible and accurate. There is much to work on.

I feel I am making progress. By tiny fractions of inches, my left hand is becoming more flexible. It is not yet really a cellist's hand, but it is beginning to look and feel more like one. Both hands are much too slow, but getting quicker. In the orchestra, in the very fast passages of the Haydn and Beethoven, I still don't get *all* the notes, but more of them than I did, and with more conviction. Much of the time, instead of guessing and leaning on the good players as I used to, I really know what I am doing. Some of our new cellists now and then even lean on me. For the first time I feel that I am actually a useful member of the orchestra—a good feeling. My sight-reading is still bad, but getting better. I can't read the cello parts to those Mozart quartets at playing tempo, but it takes me much less time to find the notes than it would have even six months ago. I am slowly learning to count, think, and play all at once. At orchestra rehearsal last night I became aware, to my great surprise and pleasure, that I was able to see more notes at once, and see further ahead. It was not a matter of *trying* to, I just could, like a child learning to read print, who can only see one letter at a time, and one day suddenly finds that he can see whole words. I knew all along that I *should* see more notes at a time, *should* look ahead, but I couldn't do it. Now, even when I am not trying to make it happen, it is beginning to happen. It is as if my eyes themselves had changed.

What pleases me most, though, is what I can hear and feel happening in my right arm, my bow arm. First of all, the bow *feels* so good in my hand. Just to hold it, or to draw it across the strings, is a most voluptuous sensation. The bow seems to nestle in my fingers, feels as if it is growing out of them, is a part of them. In practice I spend a lot of time just drawing long bows across the strings, trying to get an absolutely even tone from the frog (the end I hold on to) to the tip. This is hard, above all when playing softly, yet I come much closer to it than

I used to. Much of the time I get what my ears and even my tape recorder tell me is a nice sound.

I should do even better when I get a good cello. When I began to play regularly with my uncle's cello, I hoped it would prove to be a good enough instrument to play for the rest of my life. But it isn't and can't be; it has had too hard a life. The belly has been cracked in fifteen or more places, and even the ribs are warped and cracked. It is very hard to play; from the lowest F up two full octaves there is not just one but many notes on which I can get a "wolf," a kind of falsetto or yodel. On almost every note, if I bow lightly and quickly, which the music sometimes demands, the note jumps up an octave or more. To make the strings sound I have to dig into them harder than I should. When I play other people's instruments I realize how hard I have to work just to play my own.

Fortunately help is on the way. In Boston there is a very skilled instrument maker and repairer named Horst Kloss. I had seen him working on my cello and other instruments. I liked the way he worked, and what he said about his work. From many sources I had learned that what makes great instruments great are not mysterious lost secrets of varnish, etc., but good design, fine materials, and above all the most precise and careful workmanship. I had read that Sidney Weiss, a former concertmaster of the Chicago Symphony, had made for himself a violin which in time he came to prefer even to his Stradivarius. I had met a world-famous virtuoso bass player, and a principal cellist of a major symphony, both of whom played new instruments and an assistant principal cellist who played with one he had made himself. Clearly there were people around who knew how to make fine instruments. Horst Kloss looked to me like one of them. It seemed highly probable that he could make me a cello far better than any old one I could afford to buy. I asked if he would be interested, and he said he would be delighted. Not only that, but I could come to his shop from time to time, and watch him working on it. It has been extraordinarily interesting to see a cello built, so to speak, from the ground up. I had no idea how much delicate and painstaking craftsmanship, not to say hard physical labor, it takes to make one. When it is finished, I will enjoy it all the more for having seen what went into it.

As I try to become a skilled musician, time is my chief problem. In a book about piano playing, I once read a story about a nineteenth-century British writer, I think Matthew Arnold. Not only did he write essays, but he had many other important public positions and duties. With all this, he was an accomplished pianist. Someone once asked him how, with all he had to do, he was able to find time to practice and play the piano. He said, "I cleared a space."

Exactly. Adults who want to learn to make music well are going to have to clear a space. They are going to have to stop doing many things they have been doing, including many things they liked. To make more time for music, I have had to give up many pleasures I have enjoyed for years. This is no complaint; I am lucky to have surplus pleasures I *can* give up. I don't go any more to the ballet, which I have always loved, or to the theatre or movies, which I liked to go to once in a while. In Boston there are good concerts almost every night, often several on the same night. But outside of the Boston Symphony, which is too beautiful to give up, I go to few concerts. There are many other recreations that have given me great pleasure in the past, that I may rarely or never do again —sailing, canoeing, swimming, skiing, squash, tennis, soccer, skating, fishing, wilderness camping, mountain backpacking. I realize this without the slightest regret. I have always loved sports, athletics; they have been an important part of my life. But music is athletics, a sport more difficult and fascinating than any I have ever played. There is enough teamwork and split-second coordination in any symphony concert to fill up a

Epilogue

237

dozen Super Bowls. The challenge of teaching, coaxing, and tricking the muscles of my hands and arms into moving faster than they think they can move is even more absorbing than the many challenges of sports which have interested me for so long. There seem to be so many more kinds of problems in music, and so many more ways to work on them. It is a limitless field for thought, invention, experiment.

Friendship, another important part of my life, also has to give way. I have friends in many parts of the U.S., and in Canada, England, France, Denmark, Norway. One of the great pleasures of my life has been traveling and visiting these friends. But unless I can find a way, which I don't see now, to do this without giving up my music, I am going to spend most of my time at home. I don't even see as much as I would like of old friends who live right in Boston. I feel a little bad about this, wish I had time for everything. But I don't, so music, or friendships built around music, have to come first.

Even in music there are things I will have to give up. For years I have been exploring the world of music through recordings, borrowing them or buying them when I could afford to. I have tried to hear as much as I could of the world's great music, and also of its unknown or neglected masterpieces. In these searches I have listened to a lot of bad music, but I have also found much treasure, beautiful music that most musicians have never heard or often even heard of. Turning up these gems, and telling other people about them, has been one of my greatest pleasures. But I am beginning to see that more and more I am going to have to choose between playing and listening. I can't explore all of music, can't even hear all that has been recorded; it would take lifetimes. To produce more music, I am going to have to consume less. I already consume less than I used to, but I will have to cut down still more. This will be hard, as hard as for many people to cut down or give up TV or smoking. Of course, these little problems of mine are very small problems indeed. Most people would quite rightly not consider them problems at all. I only mention them to make the point that people who want to become skillful at making music are going to have to give up some things they like, and perhaps like very much.

Other things are not easy for me to give up. Writing, for one. In the first place it is the part of my work from which I earn most of my living. But beyond that, I am as much a writer, a man of letters, as I am a musician or would-be musician. The city, the country, the world I live in, interest me. Ideas about them churn in my mind, words pop up and and demand to be written down. Sometimes while playing the cello I will find that the main part of my mind is making words instead of music. I try to say, "I'll think about that later." It doesn't work. The mind says, "No, not later, *right now!*" After a while I give up, put down the cello, and go write down whatever I am thinking until the mind is satisfied and willing to go back to music. I am like the rope in a tug of war, the writer pulling one way, the musician another. Some say, "Why not set aside half the day for writing and the other half for music?" But both the writer and the musician want full time. When the writer is in command, working on a book or an article for my newsletter, words are in my mind all the time, music making seems remote and trivial. When the musician is in command, I think music all the time. As after playing those Haydn quartets, I hear and *feel* myself playing the music I am trying to learn. Even my fingers are thinking (so to speak) about what they are going to have to do next. Walking down the street I do hand and finger exercises. I begrudge every minute away from the instrument. Words seem a distraction. To the word maker, the music maker says, "There is too much talk in the world already, are you going to spend your whole life yak-yak-yakking at people?" It is a kind of war.

One of the things I have had to learn to do, not just to make time for music but to keep some sanity, is give up the idea that I have to know and do something about everything, or everything bad, that is happening here and in the world. To be "well informed," I used to read huge stacks of books, magazines, newsletters, newspapers, etc. Most of these I have given up. I accept, finally, that I can't know something, far less *do* something, about *everything*. I have to pick and choose. On the whole I don't read publications anymore that tell me only about outrages. I already have all the bad news I can stand. But there remain a whole host of problems and issues that seize my mind. It is not a matter of believing that these are important issues and that therefore I ought to think about them. I can't *stop* thinking about them. Such matters as how to get energy from sun, wind, waves, and other permanent sources; how to conserve materials and recycle wastes; how to use worms, plants, algae, shellfish, and other creatures to recycle organic wastes; how to grow more food on less land, and even in the city; how to make ourselves, our neighborhoods, and our towns and cities more self-sufficient; how to make our political and economic institutions smaller, and so more efficient, responsive, and manageable. These seem to me key problems. If we can solve them, learn to live in harmony with nature, get more from less and make do with less, many other problems, including unemployment and poverty, can probably be solved. If instead we go on living wastefully and destructively, nothing else we do will make much difference. But just to keep up with what is happening in these fields, and to help this work along in what ways I can, takes more and more time.

One other interest and work takes up much of my time and thought and will take still more. For many years, with many others, I tried to make schools more kindly, interesting, competent, and serious. It now seems clear that in the near future this will not happen, mostly because there are so few people, in or out of schools, who want it to happen. To those few people who can't stand what schools are doing to their children, I now urge that they look for ways to take their children out altogether and have them learn at home. To help them do this I have begun to publish a newsletter, *Growing Without Schooling*. As I write, it is still very small, with only a few more than four hundred subscribers. I hope that before long there will be ten or more times that many. But if I then get ten times as many letters on this subject as now, I hardly know where I will find time to read them, let alone think about and answer them. I may have a tiger by the tail, which in a few years will eat up my life, leaving little space for music or anything else. Time will tell.

Even if I can keep a space clear for music, time may also tell me something else—that the experts were right. Perhaps people in their fifties, like me, really do have something missing in their nervous and muscular systems that makes it impossible for them to become skillful musicians. It seems unlikely, since musicians go on playing expertly and professionally into their seventies and eighties. But maybe in my case it will prove to be so. Perhaps I will hit a speed barrier, a point beyond which I just can't make my brain, eyes, arms, hands, and fingers work any faster. Perhaps I will find that even though I learn and improve, I do it so slowly that to play as well as I would like to would take me eighteen hours a day for fifty years—hours and years I don't have. Someday I may have to say to myself, "Let's face it, John, you aren't ever going to become a skilled player, or even much better than you are right now." What then? By the time I can no longer dodge such a truth, I will have had many glimpses of it. Maybe I will be ready for it. I hope I will say, "Well, I've had a lot of fun these past years playing the cello no better than I do, so I'll just go right on playing it that way." Meanwhile, none of this has happened.

Epilogue

If Nature has waiting for me up the road some kind of impassable barrier, she has so far given me no clear signs of it.

I am full of hope. The music for Monday's orchestra and Tuesday's quartet is on the stand. Both have concerts coming up in a few weeks.

Back to work.

Appendix:
Musical Intervals

Tones—up	Music
1	do-re; *"Frère* Jacques."
1 1/2	*Marchi*ta (Marquita?); "On The Trail" (Ferde Grofé).
2	do-mi.
2 1/2	"South Rampart Street Parade"; "Taps"; "*The Po*pe (he leads a jolly life)" Tannhäuser; "*Here co*mes (the bride)."
3	First and Third notes, beginning Sibelius Fourth Symphony.
3 1/2	do-sol; *Zarathustra; "he's free* (from every care and strife)"; *"Wha*t'll I *do"* (old popular song).
4	". . . *when you* (are far away)," same song as for 3 1/2.

| 4 1/2 | N-B-(C); *"It's whis*ky (that makes the world go round)"; "Liebestraum" |
| 5 | Fragment from *The Rite of Spring;* Lohengrin Prelude, first and fourth notes. |

Tones—down

1/2	do-si; *"All through* the night" (Cole Porter).
1	"Nuages"; "Three Blind Mice"; theme, first movement Tchaikowsky Sixth Symphony.
1 1/2	Children's taunting song; cuckoo.
2	"Nuages" (second pair of notes): *"We* (three) *Kings* (of orient are)."
2 1/2	"South Rampart Street" (second and third notes); *"We Three* (Kings, upon the break of day)"; *"Bon Voy*age, M. Dubonnet."
3	Lohengrin Prelude, fourth and twelfth notes.
3 1/2	"Watch on the Rhine"; "Star Spangled Banner," first and third notes.
4	Second theme, second movement Tchaikowsky Fifth Symphony (once popular song called "Fools Fall In Love").
4 1/2	First two notes, Chopin Piano Concerto No. 2; *"Fancy* (you falling for me)," old popular song.
5	"Night Watchman" (old Woody Herman tune), first and fourth notes.

ABOUT THE AUTHOR

JOHN HOLT (1923–1985), writer, educator, lecturer, and amateur musician, wrote ten books, including *How Children Fail*, *How Children Learn*, and *Learning All the Time*. His work has been translated into fourteen languages. *How Children Fail*, which the *New York Review of Books* rated as "in a class with Piaget," has sold over a million copies in its many editions. John Holt, for years a leading figure in school reform, became increasingly interested in how children learn outside school. The magazine he founded, *Growing without Schooling*, continues to reflect his philosophy. It is published by Holt Associates, 2269 Massachusetts Avenue, Cambridge, MA 02140.